For My Son. My Reason For Living. My Reason For Everything.

Special Thanks To:
The Varr Family
The Melucci Family
The Bristow Family
The Kieltyka Family

To Renee…I don't know how you do it. But thank you for pushing me to believe and dream big.

The Job:

Sins of the Father

"Prepare for his sons a place of slaughter because of the iniquity of their fathers. They must not arise and take possession of the earth and fill the face of the world with cities."

Isaiah 14:21

1

The DOA

It was about 8:15 AM when the call came in. Human remains found inside City Park Zoo in Portside, RI. Police and rescue were notified, however rescue wasn't needed. A zoo employee had found part of a hand severed just above the wrist located inside the polar bear exhibit. The hand only had two fingers still attached. A leg was also found missing the foot. Broken shards of bone were found scattered.

It was late January 2015 and the zoo had been closed for the season, the park usually being a desolate wasteland at this time of year, although during the summer it's packed with visitors and lo-cals. Some come for its beauty. Some come sim-ply for a lazy afternoon picnic. But most come for the large zoo, located in the northwest corner of the park. It's only open in the warmer seasons, with the main attraction being the polar bear exhib-it.

By this point, several units had converged on the location and started their search for evidence. Jason McGuire of Metro PD was the first detective on scene. After being briefed by the patrol units, he walked up to the exhibit and could see other officers standing over the remains which were situated in two different areas of the polar bear enclosure. The detective was introduced to a zoo employee named Bob McLaren. Bob stood about 6 feet. He was a toothpick. He was balding and had a thin mustache. Kind of looked like a pedophile. He wore a blue one-piece with the name "Joe" on the left breast. All the best, he guessed, for city employees.

McGuire: "So, Mr. McLaren, can you tell me what happened here this morning?"

Bob: "Well I came in about 7:00 AM. Grabbed some sardines for the penguins and fed them first as I usually
do. Then grabbed some larger fish to bring up to the bear pen. I banged on the fish can a few times which usually gets them out and about. It's kind of like their signal. For some reason, they didn't respond today. So I banged and banged on the can and the railing and finally one of the cubs came out of their little cave-like area. And that's when I noticed she had what looked like blood around her mouth and chest."

McGuire: "Is that unusual?"

Bob: "Most definitely".

McGuire: "What did you do next?"

Bob: "So I called down to the office to see if someone else had fed them today but my boss said that no one had even left the office. I asked to have a few others come out so we could herd them into a separate secure pen. That's where we usually put them when we have to clean the bear shit," he said, with a look of disgust on his face.

McGuire "How many of them are there?"

Bob: "Three. A momma and two cubs, one male and one female."

McGuire: "Then what happened?"

Bob: "Well, I was real nervous when my boss said that they weren't fed yet. I thought maybe one of them got hurt or they had attacked each other. So my boss and a few others came up and we got the bears put away. All three were red around their mouths and chest and paws, but none of them looked hurt. It definitely wasn't their blood. So we started looking around and my boss found a leg on one end of the exhibit and then I found part of a hand down in the pit."

McGuire: "Did you happen to notice anything unusual or see anything else down there like clothing?"

Bob: "Well, you have to walk through a private rear access area to get to the employee entrance of the pen. There's a maintenance area over there too. When I was walking behind the polar bear exhibit, I saw a portable breathing thing. The kind used by fire and rescue people when they work on critical patients or like accident victims and stuff like that."

McGuire: "Is that unusual?"

Bob: "Well, I've have never seen one in the park before and thought it was odd, but I've only been here three months. So I picked it up and placed it in the maintenance closet behind the exhibit, figuring whoever left it would return for it. I figured it probably belonged to the zoo veterinarian or something."

McGuire: "What about clothing? Maybe a wallet? Could I be that fucking lucky?" as he chuckled.

Bob: "Nah. To be honest detective I really didn't look too hard. The smell of shit alone in there is too much for me. I didn't feel like finding anymore body parts. They say this happens every other year or so. Some drunken whacko decides he wants to swim with the polar bears and gets eaten. This is my first one though."

McGuire: "I hear ya on that one. What's your boss's name?"

Bob: "Maria Hynes. That's her over there. You might want something to cover your nose though."

McGuire had just the thing. The detective made his way through the back area. It was a skinny walkway which lead to a steel gate on the left and a small shed on the right. The gate was opened and McGuire entered, joining the rest of the group. *Fuck,* he thought to himself. *Bob was right about the stench.* He made his way over to the only female in the group and introduced himself. She was bundled up in a bomber-style winter jacket and blue jeans. It was hard to ascertain what she had packed under the layers of clothes, but her face was cute.

McGuire: "Hey, Jay McGuire. Isn't this lovely day we're having?"

Maria: "Hi, I'm Maria. And this day is anything but lovely. I haven't even had my coffee yet."

McGuire: "You are probably going to hate me, but do you mind if I spark up? I'm the worst with smells."

Maria: "Go ahead" she laughs. "I thought you cops had to smell it all."

McGuire: "Dead bodies on a hot summer day... yes. Polar bear shit and stench, however, there is no training for that."

McGuire reached into his pocket and removed a small cigar, a J Grotto Anniversary Perfecto to be exact. J Grotto was a local cigar company whose owner McGuire had befriended years earlier. Cigars were his one vice, well, cigars and motorcycles. And of course Tom Fucking Brady and his Patriots. He slowly toasted the foot of the smoke before placing it in his mouth for the final light. *Ahhhh...heaven!*

Maria: "Thanks actually. I'm gonna hang near you. I'd rather smell that all day."

McGuire: "Ease up babe. I'm a married man."

as they both laughed. "So what the hell happened? We haven't had one of these in a few years, isn't that right? Never in the winter actually I don't think."

Maria: "Yeah. Most people don't realize the bears stay here in the winter. Them and the penguins. The warm weather animals we send down to Georgia for the season. But yeah, I've been here fifteen years and I've had seven of these. Each one worse than the last."

McGuire: "So what happened this morning? How were you notified about this?"

Maria: "The new guy, Bob, came over the radio and asked if anyone had fed the bears yet. Something like the penguins ate ok but the bears weren't interested. I think he said he saw blood, too. I'm not sure. Our radios suck so I asked him to call me on his cell."

McGuire: "What does he say when he called?"

Maria: "Yeah, so he says that one of the bears looks injured and that he couldn't see the others. So I asked around and told him that everyone was saying they didn't feed them. It was too cold, no one wanted to go out. And then I looked at the video monitor from inside their cave. The others looked like they were resting. The cub was playing around with something. But they didn't look sick or nothing."

McGuire: "What's this cave?"

Maria: "Well the whole thing is man-made obviously. We don't have mountains over here. So they kinda have their own cave area built into the wall to keep them out of the elements and stuff. They usually just go in there to sleep. Most of the time they spend out in the exhibit playing and swimming."

McGuire: "Please tell me that there are cameras outside of the cave."

Maria: "I'd love to tell you that. But I cannot tell a lie."

McGuire: "Of course. Can you show me where they found the remains?"

Maria takes the detective across the pen and points out what appears to be a leg. It's severed just above the ankle and an inch or two above the knee. Then she walks him down a steep set of stone steps into the pit. The pit is a massive area with a twenty foot drop that separates the exhibit from the people, making it impossible for the bears to climb up the wall or jump across the divide. Down in the pit, Maria points out what looks like part of a left hand. The detective also notices a cell phone broken into a few pieces.

McGuire: "Would you know how long that phone has been there? Odd that there is no clothing but this person brought a phone. Maybe they took a final selfie. The victim or the bears," as he smirked.

Maria: "Har har!. Actually I wouldn't know, no one usually comes down here, except the staff or

the bears. Mostly people just throw coins over.
Phones are too expensive."

McGuire makes a mental note to have BCI
seize the phone.

"Maria" a voice yells out, "you're gonna want to
come back up here." They both respond back to
the surface and are directed into the bear cave.
As they approached an employee points towards
the rear left corner.

When they enter, they observe a bloodbath.
It's almost impossible to think that all this blood
could come from one person. Maria loses it, trying
not to vomit as she attempts to run out. *Well there
goes my crime scene.* The detective walks over,
carefully stepping to avoid the blood, which is
nearly impossible at this point.   He sees a human
head. It's unknown if it's male or female. The hair
is somewhat short. The face has been completely
eaten off.

McGuire: "Maria? Where was that cub on the
video when you said it looked like he was playing
with something?"

Maria: "Right where you are standing. In that
corner" as she peeked in with a green face.

Great…my victim's head was a bear's chew toy.

By that time, BCI, Metro PD's forensics unit arrived. Patrol units were positioned near evidence
locations as well as by the gate. Maria and Bob
responded to central station and provided witness

statements for detectives. The Medical Examiner showed up and took what he could. He informed McGuire that it would be a difficult identification, based on the condition of the fingers. The best bet would be to research missing persons and try to match dental records.

The weekend was fast approaching. McGuire checked with the Missing Persons Unit but the difficulty was that the actual sex of the victim hadn't been identified yet. Nor race for that matter. The remaining skin was so gray and ashen that it was difficult to determine if he or she was white, black, Hispanic…. And the Missing Person Unit only kept track of those missing from the city. This person could have been from any city or planet, for that matter. More information needed to be gathered at the autopsy before McGuire could proceed. Before he left the zoo, he stopped in the office and Maria pulled up video from the previous night and then set it on fast forward. They notice that around 4:30 AM, the bears seem to be awake and make their way out of the den and then don't reappear until about 6:30.

2

A Death in the Family

Monday rolls around and McGuire is late for work as usual. On his way to the squad room, his phone rings and he sees it's the station on his caller ID. He forwards it to voicemail. They always seem to call just as he enters the building. Probably his sergeant busting his balls on his tardiness. He enters the squad room to no reaction. His boss doesn't even acknowledge him. Most of the others are tied up with a homicide that came in over the weekend. He walks by Rhonda, the clerk's, office. Rhonda had been with the department for 35 years. She was a crazy old witch and she let everyone know it.

Rhonda: "Do you know what time we start around here McGuire?"

McGuire: "I love you too babe".

He enters his sergeant's office. Detective Sergeant Timothy Collins. A tall, rugged monster with a chiseled jaw and a forehead you could project a movie on. He seemed to purposely pick shirts from the kiddie section to show off his pipes.

McGuire: "You called me Sarge"?

Collins: "Nope. Maybe it was Rhonda. Or it must have been your guilty conscious. How you making out on that ID?"

McGuire: "Just got in. No calls over the week-end. Autopsy should have been finished no later than this morning. I'll check in with the ME".

He sits at his desk and pulls up his emails. Nothing new is happening. No messages are pertaining to the zoo caper. Another detective walks by and informs him that the BCI lieutenant was looking for him. *Great!!* he thought. He hated her. The ultimate kiss ass, and she was a rat fuck as well. He checked his voicemail and sure enough it was her. The Medical Examiner had gotten an ID and she urged McGuire to get to her office as soon as possible and tell no one.

McGuire starts the long walk down the third floor hallway. Several offices are to the left and right, all mostly administrative. Before he could reach the end of the hall, he goes deaf when a large pop rings out and stuns him. He's never heard a gun fired indoors so he has no idea what this is. He tries the next two doors which are locked, and then comes to the door belonging to the head of administration, Major Sergio Bucci. McGuire enters and sees that the clerk isn't at her desk. As he approaches the back left corner of the office leading to the Major's room, he can smell it....gunpowder. He immediately draws his weapon and slowly turns training his firearm on the office opening, cutting the pie as they call it. He gets about halfway through the doorway when he sees the blood and brain matter covering the wall and ceiling and still dripping. He still slowly cuts the room because he can't see to the left and doesn't know if the Major is alone. Just then, the chief of police and others including the BCI Lieutenant, burst through the room and they see McGuire pointing his firearm towards the major. The Colonel orders McGuire to secure his weapon and back off. They enter the room, but it's too late. The entire top half of the Major's head from the eyes up is gone. His white uniform shirt is now dyed red. Perfectly ironed creases down the sleeves. His badges and departmental pins in perfect order, not a centimeter off center, all now covered in brain matter. Blood continues to pour from his nose as if someone left a faucet on. His department-issued weapon is in his lap. Blood and brain drip from the ceiling onto officers trying to do what they can for whatever reason, but he's gone. The chief just stares at McGuire. McGuire, although in shock, tries not to smirk.

A Vision

I enter the room. Today is the day. It has all come down to this. My affairs are in order. Life insurance is paid up. It's my turn for justice. This fuck thought he was going to get away with this. It will be him, then the Chief. I sit and stalk him through the window. The Major's car enters the rear lot and disappears into the garage below the building. Seven minutes from now he will be upstairs and sitting in his office, after getting his coffee on the first floor. I've studied his movements for months. All I need now is for his clerk to leave for one of the fifty-odd cigarette breaks that she takes everyday. Fucking fiend. And there she goes, outside by the picnic table with the rest of the degenerates. I make my way down the hall, smiling and waving to those I pass. No one is even suspicious. I enter the room and close the private hall door that leads to the Chief's office. He will be barging through that door in a matter of seconds. I draw my weapon and call out "Major". He responds. He's there. Sitting. Not suspecting that his time has come. I turn the corner and give him no time to move. He sees my face. He has to. He has to know who is doing this. Otherwise it's meaningless. I tell him that I will give him a

chance to apologize. Apologize for what he did to
me, to my family. But before he can, I let him
know that he will still die. The apology is not for
me, it's for him. So he can make peace with what
he did. And he does, he apologizes to no end.
Fucking phony. He played with fire, now the fire is
playing with him. I let the thoughts play in his
head for a few seconds. I can see the fear. I can
smell the fear. Finally, my day has come. I place
the gun to the back of his head and BLAMMM!!
Major Bucci stew all over the desk. It's magnifi-
cent. I only have seconds to spare before the
Chief and his deputy will rush in. I can pop the
Chief, and his second-in-command will finish me
off in a full blaze of glory. But it seems like an
eternity as I stare at the blood and brains on the
desk and begin imaging shapes. It's like looking
at clouds or ink blots. I think I can see a mid 80's
Toyota. Or a steak dinner with baked potato and
corn on the cob. The possibilities are endless and
beautiful. I duck behind the desk as I hear the
door open. I can hear him calling out for the
Major. His steps get louder. I can almost taste
him. He peeks his head in and......

WTF Just Happened?

The Chief orders that McGuire's weapon be turned over immediately. He doesn't know why but complies anyway. It all seems like a dream. A dream he's been playing over in his head for years. McGuire heads back to the squad room and sits at his desk in silence, stunned.

Everyone asks him what happened. He just shakes his head. The whole building is in complete chaos. McGuire can't make heads or tails of anything. Part of him can't believe what he just saw. Part of him feels thrilled, satisfied. He hated Bucci....and the Chief. And they hated him right back. McGuire had long dreamt of this day. But he fought those urges. He did his job. He always felt that if they even sensed his hatred of them, they would win. He always made sure to smile when they passed. And to pop the most professional of salutes, even as they ignored him. He knew they would be pissed off to no end if he refused to be a malcontent or a distraction in any way. He certainly did have a right too.

Sgt. Collins came into the squad and called McGuire into his office.

Collins: "Close the door".

McGuire: "Where's my gun, Sarge?"

Collins: "I don't know. Maybe Internal Affairs has it".

McGuire: "IA? What the fuck is going on"?

Collins: "I'm sure they're going to ask you that. What the fuck happened? Did he say anything? What did you see"?

McGuire: "I didn't see anything, Sarge. I heard the pop and waited a few seconds. I didn't hear anything else. No one screaming. No one coming out of any of the offices. I tried a couple locked doors and the Major's was open".

Collins: "So you weren't in there when the shot went off"?

McGuire: "No. Are you out of your fucking mind?"

Collins: "The Chief is already commenting on the coincidence that you were the first one in, of all the people on the job. It's not like you and the Major had a loving relationship".

McGuire: "I hated the man, Sarge. Still do. But he was a cop. I know what this job is about. My dad prepped me well. I would never ever hurt any one of you guys. I'd take a bullet for all of you. Even him."

The most important unwritten rule amongst cops is that you don't fuck with someone's kid, no matter how much you dislike or go to war with their parent(s). Major Bucci didn't feel that way.

    Collins: "Well they're going to be asking you some questions. Just make sure your story is straight. You'll be okay".
    McGure: "Again with this guy? Why the fuck is this happening to me". *And why would he cap himself in his office?, he thinks,* as he gets up to leave.
    Collins: "So you didn't hear"?
    Mcguire: "Hear what, sarge"?
    Collins: "The ID from the zoo, it's Bucci's son".

5

The Departed

Patrolman Sergio Bucci Jr. was an eight year veteran of the force. He followed in his fathers footsteps just like McGuire had. McGuire didn't really know him and maybe had said "hi" to him five times in eight years. They worked different shifts. Bucci was a pretty boy. A single bachelor cop living the dream. He was heavy into body building and his image. He always kept a clean, pressed uniform. The kid looked impressive when he was out on the road. *But why? Why the fuck was he butt-naked in the bottom of a polar bear exhibit in the middle of winter?*

McGuire goes through the sham with the Internal Affairs Bureau. They're only trying to humor the Chief and he knows that. The hallway is monitored by video surveillance. Everything McGuire is saying was apparent on the footage, assuming that the shot goes off when he says it does. But it's obvious that he's stunned briefly and then tries a couple of doors before he enters the Major's office. It is also explained to McGuire that about ten minutes before he entered the hallway, the BCI Lieutenant and the Chief are seen on video leaving the Major's office. She had obviously notified him of his son's identification from the ME's office. *That stupid bitch! She told me to tell no one. They should have secured his weapon before telling him.* And no rounds were missing from McGuire's firearm. He agrees to submit to a GSR test (Gun Shot Residue), again, to humor the Chief. Afterwards, he is given back his firearm and takes the rest of the day off.

The next day he's not only on time, he's about an hour early. He couldn't sleep the night before. He needs to get to Bucci Junior's home which is only a few blocks from City Park. Bucci had been out on injury status due to a busted knee recently suffered in a foot chase. He hadn't been expected to return to work for some months so it made sense that no one had seen or heard from him. McGuire arrives at the home and notifies BCI to respond. He also contacts the fire department for a forced entry into the home. Once inside, it is apparent that Bucci was living the life. And he was a total neat freak. On one end of the living room was a bar with the most expensive liquors around, not a bottle less than fifty bucks. The kitchen was spotless with a pantry closet full of protein powders and body building supplements. The bedroom had a king-sized canopy bed. There must have been a hundred candles in the bedroom alone. McGuire found a small bag similar to the kind used as a traveling shaving kit. Inside, he found three different injectable anabolic steroids as well as two different bottles of oral steroids. He had BCI photograph the contents but he asked them to keep it on the hush. There was also a bag of hypodermic needles found in the bathroom, as well as, a few loose needles found in a kitchen drawer. It was no surprise given his physique and lifestyle that Bucci had had a little help. But there was no need to publicize it. A pill bottle was found in a dresser which later tested positive for MDMA. Again, not a surprise given the way he lived and partied. The items were apparently for personal use. He definitely wasn't pushing this shit. Different pain meds were also found, more than likely prescribed for his knee injury. McGuire searched but couldn't find any signs that Bucci was in trouble or had demons. No weird or ominous notes or messages left anywhere. Everything was as it seemed, the kid did not have a care in the world. A key to his car was found in a junk drawer in the kitchen, probably a spare. No house keys were found. The detectives searched his vehicle which was just as spotless as his house, except for an uncapped needle and syringe found between the seat and the driver's door. The needle matched those found in the house. It seemed odd given how neat he seemed to have lived, that he would have unknowingly dropped it. McGuire had it secured and seized. No cell phone was found, making it clear now that the phone found in the polar bear exhibit was probably his. But all in all, the search gave no clues as to what had happened.

Could it have been a party drug and 'roid-raged induced episode? Was it a reaction to the pain meds he was taking for his injury? Was he on the outs with a girl that no one knew about? One thing was clear, Metro PD was about to bury two of it's own. A father and a son.

6

The Biggest Little State in the Union

Rhode Island, aka Rogue Island. The Ocean State. Also known as the Pothole State. A state of rebels, for rebels, founded by a rebel. Roger Williams settled on the northern tip of Narragansett Bay in 1636, now known as Providence. He named it Providence as a haven for religious freedom. Williams was truly the founding father of the separation of church and state, although not as it's interpreted today. Williams was exiled out of Massachusetts for not following the King's religious beliefs. Williams believed in one God, but that there were many different pathways to heaven. He came to Rhode Island and soon settlers of all religious backgrounds joined him. Catholics, Jews, Puritans. He founded the first Baptist church, still standing today on the city's east side. The oldest synagogue in the country was also built in RI.

Williams felt that no government could or should dictate a person's religious beliefs, and thus Providence was born. Today separation of church and state is interpreted to mean that God doesn't exist. But that wasn't the essence on which it was founded. God's existence was never challenged,- it was considered blasphemy to do so. The separation simply meant that the church couldn't rule. And that no specific religion could be forced upon the people. So the next time some fucktard tries to ban a symbol of the good Lord baby Jesus off the lawn of a city or state property, claiming the founding fathers meant for this to be, you'll know that it's not true. It simply meant that the government could not force you to follow sweet baby Jesus or Mohammed or Jehovah. Never in their wildest dreams did our founding fathers believe that the future of this country would be controlled by atheists and the like.

When Williams first arrived, he was taken in and accepted by Rhode Island's true founders, Native Americans, among them, the Narragansetts. Williams didn't come in like the conqueror, similar to other well-known horror stories regarding the treatment of Native Americans. Instead, being the rebel that he was, he befriended them. Buying his land rather than taking it by force. Surrounding areas grew distrustful of Williams and his relations with the Native Americans and declared war on RI. He learned Native American culture and the language. In fact, Williams published a history of Native American languages including the Narragansetts - which hasn't been in existence in ages. If not for him, no one would know that any language specific to the tribe ever existed.

Williams was an abolitionist before the term
ever existed. He was staunch in his disapproval of
slavery, again being the rebel and independent
thinker that he was known to be. Years after his
death, while most of New England and the north
would be generally against slavery, Rhode Island
would reverse its position and become the leading
port in the slave trade triangle for the entire country. Led, of course, by John Brown, founder ironi-
cally of today's most left leaning college, Brown
University.

Rhode Island would continue to buck the trend
of the country's position at many times in history.
Rhode Island was the first state of the original 13
colonies to declare its independence from Britain.
It was also the last state to sign the Constitution,
refusing to sign until certain civil liberties for the
people were guaranteed in writing. To this day,
the state continues to push against popular belief
and normalcy. It is the only state in the country
that honors VJ Day, Victory Over Japan, as a paid
holiday. It is so ironic that the liberal cesspool of
the northeast celebrates the incineration of a gazillion Japanese citizens, once again going against
what would seem normal or just plain common
sense.

It is also the nanny state, and broker than broke. The state of handouts, taxing its base to death. If anyone truly wants to see what socialism would do to the country, it has a perfect case study in Rhode Island. Nowhere in the country is institutional slavery more active. Don't work. Don't go to school. Don't lift a finger to make your life better and get out of the gutter. You're not smart enough. The cards are stacked against you for one reason or another. It's not your fault. Instead, take this and that and whatever. Just remember, vote for us when the time comes because those other guys, they're gonna take all this away from you. They're going to push you to make your own way, to better yourself, to challenge us at every turn. Institutional slavery is simply a way for governments to keep certain people in their place so that those in power are never threatened with competition. So the rich stay rich and the poor stay poor and helpless. Everyone has a place in society and they you need to stay in that place.

Both political parties are ruled by that one percent. How they keep their place as a member of the one percent is the only thing that separates them - some under the guise of being helpful and understanding, some not so much. But make no mistake about it, they won't stand for their status being challenged. And the sheeple continue to fall

for it, hook line and sinker. And Rhode Island is
the birthplace of this institutional slavery. And this
need to stay in power breeds corruption.

Long-labeled the most corrupt state in the
union, Rhode Island has done nothing to shake it's
image. Year after year bigger and 'badder' politicians are made to walk the plank by the Feds.
Governors, Senators, House Representatives,
Mayors. Rhode Island is for sale. It always has
been. And through it all, the sheeple continue to
vote for the same cats. Almost like they love the
torture. Almost like they love the drama. The entire state suffers from battered spouse syndrome.
And for what? Because if you vote for those guys,
they might take your social security away. How
would you be able to live without that cool, crisp
twelve hundred dollars a month you get allowing
you to live in that spacious, palatial, roach and rat
infested high rise that you live in? How could you
go on living without us? We allow you to stay in
these gorgeous dirty diaper, death, and piss smell-
filled buildings. But if you vote for my opponent,
that high-roller lifestyle you're accustomed to will
be threatened. And they fall for it. The same old
bullshit every November.

The General Assembly, comprised of the
House and Senate, runs the state. The Speaker
of the House is more powerful than the governor.

That's the way the state is set up. They're controlled by special interest and employee unions.
Most union members statewide are right-leaning in
their views, yet they vote for the liberal parties because of the benefits and cash awarded to them
when contract talks roll around. For years the
unions have made deals with the devil in the name
of greed. They kept supporting the same cast of
criminal pols with both campaign contributions and
the even more powerful, union endorsement.
Rhode Island is that small. Everyone not a mu-
nicipal employee is related to one or at least very
friendly with one and that can sway votes dramatically.

And on and on it goes. Until there's no money
and the well is dry. Then the pols turn on those
who had singlehandedly put them in power. Running to local media and to the taxpayer screaming,
"its not our fault. It's those stinking good for nothing unions". As if the unions forced them all at
gunpoint to agree to the terms of any given contract in regards to pay and pension benefits.
These pols know damn well what they are doing.
And they assume they can just continue to tax the
people. And tax and tax. And the unions
shouldn't be held harmless in all this. Rather than
stick with the more ethical choices, the more fis-
cally conservative choices, they got greedy. They
had to know that this current system wasn't sus-

tainable. Instead of walking down the hill and fucking all the cows, they chose to run down the hill to fuck just one cow. Again, assuming that the state or municipality would just tax their way out of any crisis, and they do.

The state has already taxed just about anything possible under the sun. Wherever they can place a tax, it's done. They even taxed the ocean. The fucking ocean!! The ocean state taxes the actual ocean. The Atlantic Ocean touches around 50 different countries, and hundreds of millions of people, but Rhode Island owns it. Every last fucking drop of water. One can't swim in the ocean, in the Ocean State, without first paying a ridiculous tribute to the state. That surely must have taken care of the state's ever increasing debt, right? Nope. Didn't even put a dent in it.

But other than the aforementioned doom and gloom, the state is still beautiful, and worth visiting, even if only for a very short stay. Extremely short. Providence is thriving in the arts and entertainment. Newport.....well Newport is fucking Newport. One of the greatest destinations in the country. And if one has some extra pocket change for the Atlantic Ocean tribute, the beaches are a must see. And the restaurants. Oh dear God, the restaurants. Rhode Island, and especially Providence, has long been known as a food connois-

seurs wet dream. You can't find better food anywhere. Whether you're in Providence or along the
state's coast for the amazing seafood, you can't
go wrong. It's truly the only reason to actually live
in the state. And no matter where you go, you'll
find something for every palate. Federal Hill
boasts the greatest Italian restaurants on the east
coast. Stopping on "da hill" for a quick bite followed by a cappuccino and a zeppole at Roma is
mandatory. Providence's south side is loaded with
some of the best Dominican eats in the country.
Its west end, home to a large Guatemalan population, boasts its own great spots. The east side is
the place to be for some eclectic hoshy-poshy
spots. Outside of Providence, you have Cranston,
full of Italian eateries every square inch. Newport
is jamming, if you have the time to wait and the
coin to spend. Smaller areas like Central Falls, RI,
with its large Colombian population has some of
the best small spots in the state. You could walk
into any mom and pop restaurant in Central Falls
and eat like a king. And on the cheap too. Central
Falls and its border city Pawtucket have the best
Polish shops in the world. Visiting East Providence is like a visit to Portugal in itself. Just pick a
spot, close your eyes, and eat till you puke. RI
has the Hot Wiener, also known as gaggers or belly busters. It's a small hotdog with a snap to it and
it's in a bun covered in mustard and a heart attack
inducing meat sauce and then topped off with

onions and celery salt. You can't visit the state without trying one or four. And it must be washed down with a coffee milk. One also needs to try the clam cakes and chowder or chowdah!!

It's a state that is very community-driven based on its small size. Everyone knows everyone. And more importantly, everyone knows everything about everyone, or at least they think so. Never to let actual facts get in the way, gossip is the order of the day. Rhode Islanders will defend their neighbors to the death at the threat of outsiders. Yet when no threat exists, they'll attack each other just the same. And once you're accepted on the inside, there's no getting out. It's probably the only state you could enter and say hello to a complete stranger and get no response. Instead you'll get a look like you're fucked up. What is your angle? What is your motive? You must want something. It's ingrained in them from birth that no one is to be trusted.

So it's no wonder that those that represent the people are so fucked up. They come from the same gene pool. And all this packed into the tiniest state in the union. Full of some of the most unique personalities anyone could ever find.

But remember, they're rebels to this day, and loyal to no end. It's the last state you want to back into a corner, unless you plan on a long hospital stay. In that case, Rhode Island Hospital will be more than willing to accommodate you. As long as you're willing to wait several hours for those ahead of you with state sponsored free health care (see above).

The Bo Duke Affair

He would think of Bucci Jr in the days to come. What was he like? Why did he become a cop? They were probably very similar in a lot of ways. Maybe not. Jason began thinking long and hard about his own upbringing, and his relationship to his father.

It wasn't always easy. His parents divorced when he was young. He wouldn't fully realize till years later how devastating that was to him. But his father wasn't a deadbeat dad, not in the least. He coached his kids' baseball and basketball teams. Took them on long vacations. Never missed a holiday or birthday. Absent emotionally, but there physically for everything. Any place, any time. Jason admired him very much. While other kids were looking up to superheroes and movie stars as heroes and idols, Jason only looked to his dad. He was invincible and could do no wrong.

Growing up in the 80's, the hottest thing on the tube at the time for kids was the Dukes of Hazard. When Jason was 7 or 8, he got the news of a life-time. His father was going to be marching with the honor guard in a local parade. It might have been the 4th of July parade. He wasn't much interested in parades. But he thought it would be cool to see his dad in one. And then his dad dropped the bomb on him. The actor that played Bo Duke was gonna be the special guest. Bo Fucking Duke bitchezzz! And his dad told him that after the event, he was gonna be able to meet the modern-day legend. He was psyched beyond psyched. Looking back, he may have popped his cherry right there.

The parade begins and Jason is on the side-lines waiting for the Man of the Century to ride by. He was sitting with his father's girlfriend, later to become his stepmother, Kathy, also on The Job. It seemed like it took forever, but out of nowhere, he could hear the cheers getting louder. It was obvious something was coming towards their location. And before his eyes, good ole' Bo Duke. Sitting high in the back of a convertible. Jason didn't recognize him at first. He had a mustache. Bo doesn't have a freaking mustache! But it was him, Bo Duke, and all the glory that came with Bo Duke, the living legend. He was only in front of them for a few moments, and then continued on.

That was it for Jason. Like most kids, he was impatient, and fidgety. It was hot as hell. He was ready to go. Kathy told him to hang on a little longer. She promised they would leave as soon as dad passed by.

Soon he would hear a low rumble that grew louder and louder. What the hell could it be? Bo already went by. *But ah ha!!! Bo doesn't have a mustache. That must have been an imposter. Here he comes.* The cheers grew so loud that his little ears couldn't take it. Jason covered both of his ears for what seemed like an eternity with no member of the Duke family in sight. In the distance, he saw flags. They grew larger and moved closer. As his eyes focused, he could see police horses and uniforms.

"What the fu- heck" he thought. Those are just cops. As they got closer, he noticed his father right in front. He was standing tall, keeping cadence with the others, hoisting the American Flag. Dress blues were pressed and creased. All his pins and medals were lined up perfectly. You could see your reflection in his shoes. *What is going on? Why are these people going crazy? Bo Freaking Duke didn't get half this applause.*

Everything seemed to be in slow motion at this point. *"Could my dad actually be more popular than the Duke boys?"* he thought to himself, still holding his hands over his ears. The sound was deafening. In his imagination, every other cop marching seemed to disappear as did the crowd and the noise. All he saw was his pop. He started to scream "dad. Daddy". He wanted his father to see him standing there in the crowd so bad. He was just about to pass by, and when he was just about in a complete line with his boy, he turned his head ever so slightly and made eye contact. He gave Jason a wink and didn't break cadence. Jason was floored. My dad. Mine. A bigger hero than a Hollywood star. The memory of that wink was tattooed into his soul. He would never forget that wink. It was all his dad could muster emotionally throughout most of Jason's life. The wink was code for a hug or I love you. He would get the wink after scoring the winning basket or driving in the tie-breaking run. Anytime he would do something that Dennis approved of, or sometimes when he messed up, he'd search for that wink in hopes that everything was ok. It let him know that his dad was still in his corner, to continue to fight on.

That was it. The moment. The moment he decided to become a cop was right there on that sidewalk for him. Every cop's kid has that moment. Most intelligent cops dread the time their kids finally have that moment. But it's almost impossible to prevent.

That night he went home and dressed in all his dad's uniforms and wore his hats. Played with his billy club and handcuffs. Walked in his beautifully-shined shoes. As the years went by, that feeling never left. It only got stronger. Now his dad would come home and wake him up at midnight, telling him stories about this arrest and that foot chase. He would download a copy of the night's radio transmission on cassette tape and let Jason listen to the car chases. He'd bring him to the station and let him walk around, locking him up in a cell on a few occasions.

Jason loved every part of The Job. Loved the camaraderie. Loved the lingo. Even loved the smell of the rotten old headquarters building and substations. Whenever he'd move with his mother and brother to different locations in the city, Dennis would bid into the area car post. Picking his sons up for lunches in the police car. Letting them listen to the radio. That was his heaven. His escape. And he was with his hero the whole time.

He got into his fair share of trouble growing up, nothing illegal though. Smart as a whip, but an awful student. Not the best son. But certainly not the worse. Through it all, the highs and lows, he still had his eyes on the final prize, The Job. When he was 18, he crushed the postal exam and was hired immediately. Making great money at that age would have been enough to satisfy most people. But it wasn't about the coin or the security of a long career for him. He knew from minute one that it was only to hold him over. He'd have to wait until he was 21, but he'd be on The Job one day. Or die trying.

The Attack

Christmas Eve. A joyous time. Especially from the viewpoint of McGuire. A couple months removed from a divorce, he's now free. A bachelor living in the heart of the city. A city full of life and those with a taste for naughty things. The detective knew all the great spots. He knew enough to purchase a loft apartment in a complex directly above the city's hottest cafe and lounge. It was like fishing with dynamite for ass. Nonstop.

Even better, his ex was very understanding with the custody situation. She wasn't like some spiteful, vicious twats that care not a lick for the child. Only about hurting the father. Nope. She was great in that regard. She understood the importance of a father in the life of a child, especially a boy.

Under these circumstances, the detective couldn't possibly have a bad day. He either had his son, or had a lady. And if he struck out, fuck it, he had an Xbox.

All that changed on Christmas Eve. McGuire was at home sick. He wasn't feeling well for a number of days. But this day it finally caught up to him. A serious stomach bug which threatened the magic of Christmas morning. His son definitely couldn't come over while his doctor was spewing terms like "norovirus". *What the fuck!* That didn't stop his friends from down the hall from banging on his door from 1PM to 9PM and every ten minutes in between. It's party time.

Most were in the same boat. Most were single and didn't have their children for the night. This was their night. Ho fucking Ho! About 11:30 PM, McGuire woke up. He had some ginger ale and a couple of saltine crackers and then laid back down. Around midnight, surprised the food stayed down, the detective reached out to a few neighbors to see if they were still in or out, hoping to raid their refrigerators. He was starving and hadn't held down food for two days. It seemed like the entire third floor was two buildings down at some chic ultra liberal douchebag kind of hangout. The type of place where you have to show your copy of the Communist Manifesto to enter, not your ID. But the ass was easy and they had tapas to eat, whatever that was, so fuck it.

He made his way to the locale, literally two buildings away. He met with neighbors and friends and friends of friends. He was immediately dragged onto the dance floor which wasn't gonna happen. Dancing for him was considered a sin. Oh, he liked to watch the ladies dance and the guys make fools of themselves.   But it wasn't gonna happen. After about 30 seconds, he moon-walked his ass to the lounge area. A lovely lady asked him to hold her drink as she rocked on. As the detective was standing in line to buy the next round which included a bottle of hopefully the cold-est water on the planet, he could feel the cold sweats coming on. He took a quick sip of this con-coction he was holding. One of those pink chick drinks with like 8 liquors in it. A Rhode Island Ice Tea or a Long Island Gang Bang or a Palm Springs Douchenozzle. Whatever was cool at the time. That was the absolute worse thing that he could have done. His head immediately began to spin. Not seconds or minutes later. But immedi-ately, as if it was spiked. Looking back, as attrac-tive as the female was that handed it to him, it very well could have been fucked with by some serial rapist bartender or nitwit that bought it for her.

McGuire immediately grabbed his neighbor friend Douglas and told him that he was spazzing out and was going to leave, that he'd meet them back at the building. Doug urged him to stay so they could all walk back together. The club was closing in about thirty minutes. Jason insisted. He needed to go lie down for a bit. Maybe even try to eat something to absorb what he just ingested.

As he made it back to the residence, he noticed the lounge on the first floor of the building had already closed which was normal for them on a slow night. It was a quiet place that catered to small bands and open mic poetry nights. A real mellow crowd that usually didn't stay and drink till mandatory closing times. He could see into the large windows that the staff was cleaning and the bartenders and manager were sitting in their usual corner spot counting coin and making a list for their next liquor or food order. He tried the door but it was locked. His attempt caught the attention of Mark, the manager, who instructed a waitress to open the door. Jay walked in shook hands, hugged and wished everyone a Merry Christmas which is against the law in atheist-ville. But he knew that and loved to bust balls anyway. Mark offered him a drink on the house but he refused, telling them he felt ill and what he really thought he needed was a bite. The kitchen was obviously closed but the staff had ordered pizza upon closing. Several pieces were left. He woofed one slice down and was out the door.

As he walked through the doorway, he was blocked by a guy trying to get back into the bar. This guy was toast, like drunker than drunk. Annihilated. He mumbled something to the detective that sounded Dothraki to which the detective replied "have a nice night" or "Merry Christmas to you too buddy". Whatever it was it was not antagonizing or shit talking in any way. He then made his way along the building towards the other side where the residence entrance was. About 30 feet from the lush, was a group of about 15 people standing on the corner. He walked around the group, making no eye contact. As he passed, he heard a male voice call out "you talking shit?" He ignored this. They couldn't be talking to him he thought. Again he hears "are you talking shit?" Jay turns his head slightly to the left and could see the entire group facing him. He responds, "who, me?" At that point, the same voice states "yeah, you talking shit to my friend back there?" The detective realizes that this guy is referring to Yukon Jack standing back at the entrance/exit of the bar. He says "absolutely not. I told him to have a good night. You should probably get him home before he falls over."

Now Captain Brave Mouth begins to step closer to him, insisting that he was engaging in some sort of trash talking with Señor Drunk as Fuck. The detective insists that he wasn't and that he was just trying to get home, around the corner. As he turns and walks away, he can hear the footsteps. Not wanting to look back like a total pussy, he glances towards the large business windows beside him and could see the reflection of the group following him with Joe Douchebag leading the way. The detective at this point can see the entrance to his building and he turns around and faces the group. Now walking backwards, he reaches into his pockets and frantically feels for his electronic key fob for entry.

The group continues with Emperor Fuck Face getting closer and closer. At this point he has had enough and removes his badge and ID from his pocket and displays it for the world to see. Big mistake. Count Dickula's eyes widen, but not in a surprised frightened way. More like in a savage, blood thirsty way. Jay can't understand this. These kids look like punk rockers and stoners. Life long skateboarders and mommy's basement masturbators. These usually aren't the fighting type and never ever presented a problem in his experience and the detective worked almost his entire patrol career in the downtown bar area district. *This must be a joke.* But obviously this guy is having a bad day or week or life. He's bombed out of his mind and he wants to hit something. No one else in the group is talking, but they're still approaching.

The detective was warned about this drunken element. Years earlier in the police academy. The staff warned everyone that nothing good ever happens in downtown after midnight. EVER!!

The Job

One of the lessons specifically taught was that sometimes identifying yourself is not a good idea. Sometimes it incites rather than de-escalates. Sometimes drunk and disorderly fuck-wads would love nothing more than to beat the fuck out of a cop. In all his years, he was assaulted numerous times by shitheads with beer muscles. But that was always in an on duty capacity. Never off duty. *What the fuck was going on here?*

He soon realized that he has backed himself up too far into the wall. The badge and ID didn't work. And he could see peripherally that one or two subjects were circling around to the back side of each shoulder. As the big mouth got to within striking distance, the detective had no other choice. One or two is a fight. But he felt too weak and knew that he can't take on this entire group. The last thing he remembered is getting down on one knee and reaching for his off duty weapon which was holstered to his left ankle.

He awoke who knows how long or soon later, face down in the cobblestone. Making his way to his feet, he sees nothing, knows nothing. He doesn't feel hurt but he does sense something is terribly wrong. McGuire hears a female voice screaming "gun". He looks towards her with blurred vision and sees that she's standing over something. He rushes over to her and sees that she's actually standing on top of his wallet with badge and ID. He reaches down to get it and sees what looks like a gun just inches away. He doesn't recognize it at first, but knows it ain't good and she won't move. He pushes her aside and grabs the firearm, finally finding his fob and running into his house and immediately notifying an officer via cell phone to respond with a sergeant.

As he waits he feels something heavy in his pocket. He reaches in and pulls out a gun, already forgetting that he picked up a gun on the street. He then reaches for his own weapon and sees that it's not in his holster. *"Oh shit"* he thinks, *"this was my gun she was standing over, how did they get it?"*

Several units respond to the scene. The first units including a supervisor, actually observe a drunken crowd high-fiving and patting themselves on the back, bragging about just having kicked the shit out of a cop. It's clear to those that arrived that these assholes knew McGuire was a cop, and attacked him anyway. The OIC, Officer in Charge, arrived. A Lieutenant. As is policy with all off-duty incidents, the Chief of Police wants to be notified immediately. Especially if the officer is injured.

It's clear by all on scene, especially those that know Jay, that he's hurt, bad. The Lieutenant thinks he's drunk. But some of these guys know Jay. They know him all the way back to his drinking days. They knew he could handle alcohol and knew how he acted when drunk. Never ever angry. Just funnier and goofier and more perverted than ever. This was not drunk Jay. They let the Lieutenant know this. All of which should have been evident to the boss due to the plum sticking out of the detective's forehead.

The Lieutenant called and woke the Chief up at home and told him that they had had an off-duty detective involved in an incident and that he was hurt pretty badly. The Chief said he would get dressed and respond to the hospital immediately. Before hanging up, the good Chief asked the Lieutenant who the detective was. The Lieutenant didn't refer to the detective by his first name, he simply responded by saying "it's McGuire's kid". "Who?" the Chief asks. "McGuire. The retired Major. It's his kid". The Chief immediately hangs up the phone and calls and notifies the head of Internal Affairs who at the time was a Lieutenant. Lieutenant Sergio Bucci.

Bucci responds to the scene and is filled in by officers and supervisors on scene, appearing to ignore the evidence gathered. It's clear Bucci has his orders. He gathers as many from the crowd of drunken assholes as he can and he piles them into his car. He orders other officers to bring the rest of the group to his office. None are in hand-cuffs. Just what did the Chief tell Bucci on the phone? The Chief never responds to see the detective in the hospital.

9

Narcissist [nahr-suh-sist]

1.   a person who is overly self-involved, and often vain and selfish.

2.   Psychoanalysis. a person who suffers from narcissism, deriving erotic gratification from admiration of his or her own physical or mental attributes.

3.   Colonel Samuel Feldman.

Portside wanted change. It got it. Big time!!

Recent years had seen Portside become the liberal cesspool of the country. And with that came major changes. Of course all these changes were disguised with spin and soundbites and false promises. City Hall was still for sale, but the method had changed. Instead of money lining the pockets of city administrators, now the city administrators were dishing out piles of cash while demanding loyalty, obedience, and most importantly, votes.

The next 10 years would easily be the most corrupt in Portside's history, if only one was to open their eyes and not buy the bullshit and rhetoric. The local newspaper, in fact the only newspaper, was a leftist spin machine. Now that their "agenda" had seized power, they would ensure its survival with spin and information control. Negative stories were buried. Investigative journalism no longer existed. And when they couldn't help the mayor, they would publish an article pointing out flaws with his predecessor. 10 years worth of blaming this former mayor went on, all while the city gets deeper in debt, crime increases, and schools cease to exist.

The major beneficiary of this spin and media protection was the new Mayors choice of police chief, Colonel Samuel Feldman. Before going any further, it should be noted that Feldman was never a cop. EVER!! Feldman was a New York City left wing cop-hating terrorist, raised with a silver spoon in his mouth, and an attorney by trade. Also a pussy. The kind of guy who got bullied his whole life and was just waiting for the chance at revenge.

He demanded respect, but didn't earn it, and never received it because he attempted to rule by fear. But anyone that met him could see right through him. If you uttered "boo", he'd hide under his desk. He knew who to bullshit and how to suck ass. And he knew who he could push around. Even with his family. He had a wife and 4 children, none of whom could stand him, and they let it be known. His oldest child, Brandon, was adopted. He was constantly in trouble. Between alcohol and heroin it was a wonder the kid lived as long as he did. Constantly being picked up by the police and driven home on the "hush", he would always elude to dark secrets from within the home but he would never elaborate. Most took it as him just acting out.

Feldman aligned himself with major police politicians the world over. That's what modern policing had become. Gone was the past where a police chief started his career on the bricks, working in every unit the department had. Kicked in doors. Got his or her ass kicked. Stood by dead children waiting hours for the Medical Examiner to arrive. Nope, the new police administrator is brought in and groomed from day one on the job. Not worth shit as a street cop, but a great test taker. With a PhD in ass kissing and bullshittery. Now police chiefs had contracts, expense accounts, unlimited balance city-provided credit cards. Now police chiefs traveled the country and sometimes the globe for what seemed like a never-ending circle jerk. "Hey, you come to my event and tell those in my state that I'm the greatest police chief in the world. Then I'll go to your state next month and do the same".

They all joined PERF, a police administrators wet dream. A board full of blowhard politicians who help facilitate this never-ending we are the Masters of the Universe orgy. All on the public dime. These chiefs don't reach into their own pockets and eat at hot dog carts anymore. It's now all steakhouses and seafood. The type of places where you have to pay extra for a baked potato or a fucking ice cube. It has become a money-making machine.

And no doubt some chiefs have earned it. But Feldman was the worse. HE WAS NEVER A FUCKING COP!! He did have national connections though. He used his PERF jerkoffs to have the DOJ come into Portside to investigate the PD. He did this a month before it was announced he would take the job. They found nothing, naturally. But for 8 years he and that lib-tard newspaper would bring up the fact that Portside was under DOJ investigation when he came in and that he turned the place around. He, of course, didn't realize that while his friends in Washington authorized the "inquiry", they didn't come out themselves. Your natural everyday field investigator came out. Yes, they're feds, but they're still human. They were average Joe's who confided in those on the inside that this was bullshit and setup for "whatever reason". But the charade went on.

The Job

Feldman was not a dumb man by any means. Ivy League educated. He had the ability to split others. Divide and control. He came into the department and felt out the guys for a while. He decided who would say yes to him, they were all promoted. He decided who had a spine and alienated them to the point that they left. Most had enough time on the job anyway. Major Dennis McGuire was one of those guys. Although his retirement was actually planned 2 years before the Chief's arrival, Feldman insisted that he forced him out.

He gave an electronic fob device to the local police beat writer giving her full access to every room in headquarters. The paper thought he was the Messiah. Anyone involved in law enforcement for any amount of time knows that the press and police don't mix. There is not enough police can do in a positive light that is news-worthy. While the slightest fuckup is front page, above the fold. But again, this wasn't policing. He wasn't a cop. He was a politician. And they were going to sing his praises on a daily basis no matter how phony the story.

He'd visit shooting victims in the hospital. Not just any shooting victims, but actual gangbangers. Even after being made aware that some of these kids had two or three bodies on them of their own.

But who was waiting outside the emergency room? The press. The photo ops of him climbing in the back of rescues and kissing drug dealers on the forehead. The newspaper photographer who waited for hours after the burial of a fallen officer to take photos of Feldman filling the grave with a shovel and saluting. Why was the photographer there? The services had ended hours earlier. Who told him to stay? Yet he couldn't respond to the hospital for ONE of his own. He responded to the hospital on numerous occasions for other officers and gangbangers. But not for McGuire. Why?

Time went on and his reign lasted longer than it should have. Every Tuesday he'd hold a staff meeting with community "leaders" and media present as he scolded his top brass in their presence. Before entering the room, they would have to walk by a sign honoring a former colleague of his. The sign read something to the effect of how this douchebag rid the department of decades of corruption under the former city hall administration. It's funny though, that every single member of his command staff would walk by that sign every Tuesday. Some even more frequently during the week but none would utter a word in protest. All pussies. He was talking about them. Every last one of them came on during the past administration. Every last one of them had been promoted under the past administration. Most contributed heavily to the campaigns of the past administration. He was calling them cocksuckers to their faces and in public. Not one word in protest. Why? Those PERF connections brought in quite a lot of federal coin. He bought these motherfuckers. They sold their souls to his bullshit. And when he pissed in their mouths, they smiled and asked for more.

He was a bully in the truest form. Years and years of feeling inadequate, but now he was in charge. It was payback for a lifelong of stolen lunch money and bloody lips. Those that ran the local Democrat machine lauded him. He could do no wrong. Most that didn't have a dog in the fight found him repulsive though. There were countless stories about him refusing to pay for coffees and lunches. A thousand stories of him walking into some of the state's finest restaurants and de-manding an immediate seat during a two hour wait. He was the king of "do you know who I am?" He was once hosting a gathering of his PERF bud-dies and took them to the city's most exclusive restaurant without reservations. Upon entering, he told the hostess to clear the entire left wing of the restaurant, even as people were eating. She laughed in his face naturally and he exploded, "DON'T YOU KNOW WHO I AM?!!!" A very calm and collected hostess whispered "I don't give a good fuck. Take your party elsewhere".

He was hated by local mom and pop shop owners up and down the state, too. He preached
community relations. But he shit on everyone he
met while not in the presence of a news crew. He
gave speeches on passive and aggressive corruption. He would say that if you expected a free coffee, you were engaging in aggressive corruption.
He stated that if you were offered a free coffee
and accepted it, you were engaging in passive
corruption and that he saw no difference between
the two. Yet a guy who came into the job with serious bank refused to pay for anything. And if he
was made to pay, don't expect a tip. In fact, every
car in front of your business is about to get tagged.

He controlled crime statistics which helped to
fuel part of his legend. He brought in an antiquat-
ed and faulty reporting system and instituted
COMPSTAT. Every year he would release the
city's crime report and would be hailed as a hero
for the drops in numbers. The odd thing was that
the cops didn't feel like they were doing any less
work. And certainly the city residents didn't feel
any safer even during eight straight years of reported drops in crime.

The only glamorous statistic anyone was truly
concerned with was of course homicide. So even

in the event that robberies or sexual assaults went up from the previous year, he would point to the homicide rate which woulb be lower than ever. This was absolute bullshit. There is not a police chief or cop for that matter in the world that could control the murder rate. It's not possible. And gun control nuts can spew their talking points. It doesn't matter how it's done. Murder is murder. If they don't have a gun, they'll use a knife. Or a ligature. Or a blunt object. Or their bare hands. Some evil bastards are born with an instinctive primal condition for murder and they can't be stopped. If someone has murder in their blood, it's gonna happen. And they usually don't announce when or where it is going to happen. Murder shouldn't even be counted in the crime rate. It is the most uncontrollable, unpredictable crime.

Most modern crime reporting systems are linked directly to the FBI to track and sometimes predict crime. The feds also use this data to determine which cities are in need of federal coin to help combat certain crimes. Feldman didn't need the FBI for his grants or brass buyout money. He had what he needed through PERF, DOJ, ATF, and the good ole' District of Columbia. It wasn't until a few years after he was unceremoniously forced off the job, like he had done to so many others, that everyone realized the true extent of his deceit.

As the city was going bankrupt after years of mismanagement from his mayor and the shit-show he personally left behind, the department began looking for federal grants to help fund staffing and overtime and other directed enforcement type projects. Grant after grant kept getting turned down until finally the feds said look, you guys don't need the money. According to the FBI, your city has seen drops in numbers across the board of historical proportions. What?? Wait a minute!!! Something had to be wrong. These cops were more overworked than ever before. This had to be some sort of a mistake. But according to the feds, every week the completed reports got batched and sent over to the FBI for analysis. Every completed report. COMPLETED! Uncompleted reports do not get transmitted. What constitutes an uncompleted report? Forgetting to check any one of 30 or 40 mostly hidden boxes in the report itself.

An audit of the system was performed for the first time in 8 years. Tens of thousands of reports were still there at headquarters, stuck in cyber-limbo. This is how this motherfucker did it. For years people speculated that he had his minions breaking into already completed reports and changing the classifications from felony to misdemeanor, from misdemeanor to violation. But that wasn't it. It was in the junk computer program he had installed. Even as cops begged him for years to switch to the IMC program, used by every other department in the state.

He knew that mistakes would be made. He knew that mistakes were made. And he did nothing to correct them. As far as the stats or the feds were concerned, this crime or that crime never happened. He fucked the city like no politician ever had. The tougher hit economic areas knew the streets weren't getting safer. The cops knew it. And this is how he did it. This fucking disgrace of a human being.

10

A Vision

Feldman would be so easy to abduct. He always traveled alone and very rarely carried a firearm. Some police chief huh? He could be grabbed, knocked out and gagged in a matter of seconds. Bring him to an isolated place and then the real work could begin. Placing him in ancient and archaic torture devices like the rack and the Spanish Donkey. Maybe finish him off with the Judas Cradle. Or better yet, a little rat torture as a single rat slowly eats through his chest from front to back. Then dissect every part of his dead body. Scatter his limbs around the police station. Send his head through the mail to his family. Mail his cock to the Mayor.

11

The Visions

The injuries McGuire sustained that night were not fully realized right away. It would take years. One major side effect were the God awful dreams. Nightmares really. So vivid and surreal. Sometimes he would wake up and was positive that what he dreamt about actually happened. He would jump out of bed and run to the windows, peeking through the blinds to see if the cops were there or he listened for sirens.

And his thoughts tormented him. Sick thoughts. He began to fantasize about serial killers and the macabre. Most of these dreams or visions were preceded by an oncoming migraine combined with these potent powerful pain meds that came in preloaded syringes. The migraines would be so bad at times that he would vomit profusely. He was left to only take meds via injection when in the middle of a bad spell.

Some of the time he wasn't fully asleep when the visions would occur. But they seemed so fluid and carefully scripted. Almost like they were his true thoughts coming to the surface. That scared the shit out of him. Could he do murder? Did he have some dark deeply hidden desire to kill?

He would often fantasize about being Jack the Ripper, even going so far as to being time specific. By himself. Roaming the streets of late 1800's Whitechapel. Slowly and meticulously carving up his victims. Collecting organs as keepsakes. Sometimes he would apply his Ripper thoughts to modern day RI or anywhere. Could it be done? How could he get away with it? What mistakes were made?

He would dream of being the proprietor in The Castle of Dr. H.H. Holmes in Chicago in the 1890's during The World Fair. Slowly stalking his victims throughout the labyrinth he built specifically as a killing machine. Gassing his victims before dropping them in his basement, and slowly skinning them and bathing them in acid, producing perfect skeletons. It wasn't horror. It was art. He turned murder into a business. Sometimes he would imagine himself as some vigilante guest of the Holmes Castle. Quietly stalking Holmes as he himself was being stalked. Killing him in the same fashion as he would his victims. But instead of gassing Holmes, he'd skin him alive before pouring what was rest of him in acid. Or just place him in the tub of acid whole, slowly, feet first.

Where did Albert Fish go wrong? How did he get caught? This fuck was so twisted, he would get off sexually at the sight of the pain he caused his victims or even when the pain was inflicted on himself. He drove close to 29 needles into his groin at some point in his life and never removed them. They were only discovered upon his death. Could he do what Fish did? Probably not as he didn't like pain, and certainly couldn't get an erection off of it. Or would he find a way to torture Fish to the point that it was no longer sexually enjoyable? To the point that he was begging for a bullet to the head?

What if the tables were turned on Holmes, or Gacy, or Bundy? He was still a cop of course. He couldn't kill for fun. But revenge? Employing every method of death and torture that they dished out on their victims. Could he sit there like Gacy, eating dinner with his mom while the putrid odor of rotting corpses permeated through the house? Could he actually host a neighborhood cookout and serve the meat of a missing child to his unsuspecting family?

And Feldman. Sawing him slowly from the balls up. Maybe a slice a minute. Would he stay alive long enough to feel enough pain to the point of Jason's satisfaction? Would he apologize to McGuire and beg for his life? Bucci would be worse. For Bucci, no amount of begging would help. It would be some crazy Saw film type shit. Where he was actually killing himself through some twistedly rigged device. And it'd be in a public setting for all to see. It wasn't murder. It was art.

The thoughts came often and without mercy. Mostly his thoughts were directed at criminals, in a Dexter type way. But also his tormenters. He would watch the national news and see of horrific murders being committed across the country. He could go there, he thought. He could track these motherfuckers down and slaughter them in droves. He'd be the people's hero. Loved, the world over.

He'd have these visions sometimes after being given a dirty look or being cut off on the highway. Sometimes for no reason at all. This is when he was at his darkest. He was scared to death of himself and what he was capable of doing. Of what he wanted to do. Were these thoughts actually desires? Or was this normal given the circumstances? For everyone suffering a severe brain injury it was different. For him, these are the thoughts that slowly pushed him towards suicide if only to save the lives of others.

12

A Cop's Cop

Dennis McGuire was on the job 31 years. Making it to the rank of Major, in the number 2 spot at one point. Dedicated, loyal, and strict. A former Army officer, he took pride in his dress and appearance. He loved the uniform, spending all 31 years in the Patrol Bureau. He had no desire for detectives or narcotics investigation. True professional would be an understatement.

He loved his job. He loved the men and women that worked for him. Though he had zero tolerance for misbehavior, he wasn't a robot. He understood that cops, like all people, had personal lives. And demons. While he earned a reputation as a hardass, less was known about his eagerness to reach out to those cops in need. Even if he didn't know them personally. Again, if a guy fucked up while in uniform with a civilian, you wouldn't want to bear the brunt of his wrath. But if you were having genuine problems, he'd help you out. He'd set up doctor's appointments for guys needing psychotherapy or for substance abuse. He'd hook guys up with some of the best divorce attorneys. These outsiders knew one thing, keep their mouths shut. These doctors and lawyers and treatment facility connections that he had contact with knew confidentiality was key and that no one on the job could get wind of an officer's personal struggles or they'd be thrown in the rubber gun squad.

Dennis did more to keep cops out of internal affairs. Not if a cop was a shitbag. But the good ones. The honest ones. The ones who stumbled and needed a boost. While best known for the two or three cops he had fired; he was lesser known for the careers he protected, the lives he saved, and the police families he comforted. That's the way he wanted it. The position of Uniform Commander requires a hard ass, not a softy. This is the part that was never spoken of. Mainly because he asked the cops to keep silent.

But boy did he love that job. He was one of 6 children, 5 boys and one girl. Raised by a single mother who liked to dabble with beverages, they were poorer than poor. At times, they were removed from the home and sent to group homes and orphanages, they constantly bounced around. Every one of them on their own, they had to fight physically and mentally. One of the state-subsidized group homes they went to was truly the residence of the boogeyman, the Woodhaven Boys Home. It was closed years later after investigations revealed countless incidents of sexual, physical, and mental abuse as well as for a series of murders. It is something that none of the McGuire siblings would ever speak of. And it was known by all never to ask.

Another child left behind at the Woodhaven Home was Danny. Danny had a last name but to all who knew him, it was McGuire. Danny befriended the kids while a resident at the home and never left their sides, bouncing around from house to house within the family as they got older. He was like the McGuire family's very own Tom Hagan. Although he wasn't an attorney, and far from consigliere material. He was slow. Forrest Gump was a genius compared to Danny. But his handicaps were only mental. Doctors would later say that it was severe head trauma from all his beatings at the center as well as abuse at home as a child. Danny's entire family was murdered by his father. It's a miracle he survived. His father would beat and rape him, his mother, and his three siblings on a daily basis. One day, in an angel-dust induced psychosis, he doused the family in gasoline-soaked clothes and lit them on fire. Danny was the only one to survive, buried underneath his family. He suffered 3rd degree burns to most of his body and was in a coma for 4 months as he recuperated from smoke inhalation which cut off oxygen to his brain. All at the age of 3.

The Job

As he grew physically, he was a bull. He would lift the backs of cars three feet off the ground for fun. Always there when you needed a hand to help move. A pure heart of gold. No one could ever say they heard him complain or bitch about anything. Even as he would beat the ever loving fucking shit out of people that picked on his McGuire family, he'd do it with a smile. After befriending him at the home, he would become very protective of them. Anyone that he would catch fucking with the family would be attacked. And not simply knocked around, but hospitalized. And that was one of the reasons they kept him around when they were younger. That, and they couldn't get rid of him even if they wanted to. But you'd never know it by the looks of him. Always smiling. Always whistling and humming. And very religious. All the McGuire's were.

Life went on and from the ashes they rose. Every last one of getting through school and landing great jobs, all government. Public service seemed to be a calling to them. Some were firefighters. Some were police. One was career military and the other a postal worker. At the time, it was all that was available to grunts. They didn't have the money for Ivy League schools. Not even state run schools. So all got into civil service in some capacity and as a way to pay for college.

Dennis' desire was a little different though. He was a partier as a teenager. Hair down his back. Care free. Until one day he was at the local Irish pub. The place was packed and Dennis arrived with a friend. An African American friend. Irish Willie Jones. Now this was an old Irish hangout, in Portside's Irish neighborhood, in the 70's. But Willie was always welcome at The Tap. He was one of the guys. Not remotely Irish, but he was nicknamed Irish by the drunks. Sometimes called O'Jones or McJones. Willie was a great guy and one of Dennis' closest friends.

Prior to their arrival, there was a call for a dis-turbance at the bar. Usually scrums were handled in-house. These were hard-working, hard-drinking Irish folk. Enemy versus enemy. Friend versus friend. All fights ended with a hug and a shot of whiskey. This time the cops show up, two rookies. They arrived huffing and puffing, chests stuck out. They made it known that if they had to come back, batons would be flying.

About an hour later, there's a small argument outside. Just a little pushing and shoving. No one on the inside is even aware of it. Cops get called again and in barges Officers Douche and Bag. They push people around a little and scan the room. Simultaneously they lay eyes on Willie. They begin to salivate and drag Willie out of the bar and beat him to within an inch of his life. You can probably guess why he was chosen. Dennis jumps on one cop's back and the entire pub exits and beats the cops from one end of the block to the other. Backup units arrive from all over the city. By the time it's all sorted out, the street is full of beaten and bloody drunks, but only one arrest is made, Willie.

That was it for McGuire. Although typically a rebel, he was always a thinking man. A problem solver. He made up his mind right there on the spot that he was going to become a cop. And not because he liked them, but because he despised them. Despised them for what they just did to his friend. The next morning, after chopping off his lion's mane, he was at the Army recruiting center. Portside PD wasn't accepting applications at the time and it was well known that military service was a plus when applying. Dennis went from stoner to hero and joined the military to help him become a cop simply for revenge. But not physical revenge. He was thinking that he would become an officer and eventually rise in rank. Rise to the rank where he would have enough authority and influence to change things. Change things for the better in honor of Willie. Corny as shit. But that was the reason. It wasn't money. Or benefits. It was deeper than that for him.

He was stationed mainly in Germany throughout his military career. There he met his first wife,
a lovely Spaniard named Antonia. Soon she was
pregnant and Jason was born right there in a military hospital in Germany. Shortly after arriving
stateside, they had their second child, Steven.

Dennis breezed through the police academy
both physically and academically. As a rookie, he
was immediately recognized as a rising star. Nonstop arrests. Guns, high speed pursuits. He was
all over the place. He passed every promotional
exam he took. Made sergeant, then lieutenant.
Eventually becoming the youngest captain ever.
He would later become a major. Throughout his
career he realized one thing. He was wrong.
These guys and gals weren't what he thought.
They weren't that bad. Every agency has bad ap-
ples. He and Willie had obviously met two of them
years earlier. But being on The Job, he realized
the good core of the group was honest and hard
working. He came to realize that police officers
are human first. That's what everyone always
seems to forget.

The police department is just a reflection of society at any given time. The 60's and 70's
spawned race riots across the country. Rhode Island wasn't immune to that. But as time went on,
as society and people in general began to have a

better understanding of one another, he could see the change. What happened outside the department also happened on the inside. This one white man's war to end racism from the inside out never happened because of anything he did. He saw it change all on its own. Progress is cool.

As years passed, he saw two of his brothers join the force. He also met his second wife, Kathy, on The Job. Years later, Jason would join his dad amongst the ranks. Dennis saw the change coming. The job, just like any other police department, was always political. But he saw the new age of police politics on the horizon. The days of being no-nonsense cops were dwindling. Actually arresting criminals was now being frowned upon. He saw the end. He set a date for retirement. A date that would include his time served as well as his military time in order to reach a certain plateau for his pension. The date was in three years. And nothing was going to stop him from leaving. Not a promotion to chief or commissioner. Nothing.

Dennis had recently discovered the game of golf and had his eyes set on 18 holes a day, 7 days a week. He didn't even plan to put his law degree to good use. About a year before his retirement, a change came. The change he envisioned. And it wasn't good. That change was Chief Feldman. Dennis was from the old school.

A cop's cop. Feldman went through the command staff and soon realized who would be his yes men and who had to go. Dennis was the furthest thing from a yes man this Chief was ever going to see. He always believed in the chain of command and following orders for the good of the public and the department. But he wouldn't tolerate a bullshit order, even from the Chief.

13

The Feud

Times were testy. One day the Chief called him into his office. This was one of the "feeling out" days. Dennis knew what to expect because he had already been warned by others who had gotten the spiel from the Chief. Dennis thought he was different though. These other guys were big time political machines and campaign contributors to the last administration. Dennis was nobody's pawn. He had no allegiances for or against. Surely this meeting with the Chief would go differently.

The meeting begins and BAM!!. The Chief starts hurling insults. Personal insults. Calling Dennis' character and career into question. Dennis takes it for a minute, warning the Chief that he's going way below the belt, and that he is crossing the line. Inside the room is the Chiefs most trusted confidant. A retired cop that the chief brought everywhere. Dennis keeps looking at this guy, hoping he interjects. Surely once having been a cop this guy has to know what the Chief can and cannot do. What he can and cannot say.

See, what he learned early on in the military

was that respect was a two-way street. Basic training is one thing. There, you're going to get ridiculed or spoken down to and humiliated. They're trying to make men out of boys. But after that, it ends. That Full Metal Jacket shit goes out the door. Rank or no rank, you don't attack some-body personally. It is conduct unbecoming. Rank goes out the door and you can bet your ass that the subordinate can dish the same shit out to you once you've crossed the line. If you tried to bring him up on charges you'd be fucked.

Well, the Chief continues on this tirade after be-ing warned, even going so far as to bring up the Major's son. What was said Dennis doesn't com-pletely know because by this time he was shouting as well. But when he hears the word "son", he snaps. He lunges across the desk. He doesn't reach out for the Chief or attempt to touch him in any way. He simply tries to get in his face. He never has the chance to because the Chief push-es off the desk while sitting in his wheeled chair, slams up against a bookcase behind him, and smashes his head.

The Chief stands up and both Dennis and the Chief's pal can see the pee stream running down his left leg, growing in size. His bottom lip shaking uncontrollably, he lashes out...

"You can't talk to me that way. Don't you know who I am?"

"Yeah" McGuire responds, "you're a total piece of shit. Don't you ever in your fucking life threaten me or my family again".

Feldman says "I'm the Chief of police, I can say whatever I want. You're gonna be arrested for assault".

Dennis mockingly turns around and places his hands behind his back. The Chiefs right-hand man is in between them at this point had he demands that McGuire leave the room. McGuire slowly puts his hat on, mockingly salutes the Chief, and exits stage left. As he's leaving, he hears the Chiefs confidant tell him "you can't talk like that to him. You can't talk like that to anyone. What the fuck Sam?"

Weeks go by with nothing said between Dennis and the Colonel. At some point, a new police academy is scheduled to start. The recruits had been chosen from an application process long before Feldman's arrival. 4 days before the first class, Feldman has letters sent out to the selected recruits and advises them that the academy will be postponed indefinitely. Secretly, Feldman and the new Mayor select separate recruits with political affiliations from the overall application list. These recruits are told to respond to the police academy in 4 days. The academy is going to commence as planned. Except, it's going to begin with a totally different group. McGuire hears of this and flips his lid. This can't be done. These kids knew months in advance when the class was supposed to start. They've all quit their previous jobs in anticipation. In fact, Federal labor laws do not allow for a municipality to subject people to a psychological exam without an offer of employment made first. The only way they can't get the job now by law is if they failed the exam or dropped out of the academy.

Dennis does some research and gets the original list from the academy class. He also contacts a close lawyer friend. McGuire spends hours and eventually contacts every member of the original class and advises them of Feldman's plan. He also places them in contact with the attorney. Before the end of the day on a Friday, the lawyer files a motion to stay the beginning of the class which is to begin on Monday. The Chief gets the notice from the courts and loses his mind. Again, his argument is that he is the Chief and that he can do whatever he wants. This doesn't go over too well with the Judge.

Feldman is forced to reach out to the members he axed. He promises them that if they forgo a lawsuit, he would ensure that they were in the next class. Some agree, but some don't. Some can't get their old jobs back. Some simply don't feel like waiting. Years could pass before the next academy. Those that continue with the suit win easily.

That's it as far as Feldman was concerned. The McGuire family is now marked.

14

Woodhaven

The turn of the century brought the lovely idea of Eugenics. To breed out what the government determined were the feeble-minded. Locking them up in asylums until they died. Not allowing them to breed or blend with the outside world. Though this country didn't invent the concept of genetic manipulation, it sure has had its fair share of some of the worst ideas in history. Naturally the United States moved as far away from this practice once the world's greatest genetic controllers, the Nazis, were exposed. But the damage was done.

Prisons disguised as hospitals and asylums were set up across the country to house the unwanted. One of RI's most famous was the Woodhaven Boys Home. Anyone determined to be "undesirable" due to one handicap or another, mental or physical, was sent there. It also became the landing spot for children with no diagnosed disabilities, but simply because they were poor and from broken homes. Those that made it out would speak of its horrors for years. Lack of food. Lack of care. Lack of medicine.

The Job

In the 1950's numerous investigative reporters would attempt to enter undercover posing as state employees. They would report of major physical and psychological abuses. Children with obviously broken limbs that were left unsecured and without restraints. The lucky ones wore torn rags. The others wore nothing. No working heat except for in the administrative offices. Children were observed lying in piss and shit, some even engaging in coprophagia. For those that don't know, that means to literally eat feces (look it up). The chance of catching Hepatitis was 100 percent. The shell of the now abandoned building still gives off the most awful urine and shit odors.

Yet none of this spoke to the horrors committed by the staff and administrators. Children used as punching bags. Limbs broken. Some that entered healthy, left the building years later paralyzed for no other reason than being victims of abuse. Forcing patients to drink their own urine or the urine of others just for fun. Forcing patients to fight each other, even placing wagers on the contestants.

And it was a pedophile's dream. None escaped the sexual assaults. They all happened in the dark room. And not a photographer's dark room, but a room with no windows and no lights on. The boys were told that they were going in for checkups. They would leave the room and be brought straight to a private staff shower room and hosed down. They could feel the excruciating pain in their backsides and could see what seemed to be the never ending flow of blood as it worked its way towards the shower drain. None of them would know until years after their release that this type of thing didn't happen at a normal "check up" with a doctor.

Death was frequent, but because Woodhaven was labeled a health facility, autopsies were seldom conducted on the deceased because they died under a "doctor's care". Otherwise it would have been obvious that some deaths were not natural and caused by physical injury. Sexual abuse would have been obvious at autopsy as well as signs of sterilization.

Places like this existed all over the country. It was a sign of the times. Some parents couldn't care for these children. Some parents didn't want these children. Some parents were just drunken fucking losers.

The McGuire boys ended up at Woodhaven for a brief time. They were a tight knit crew and weren't gonna be pushed around by anybody. Even at that age, if you messed with one, you messed with them all.

The Job

Shortly after arriving, they noticed that one boy in particular would be signaled out and beaten more than the others. He was large for his age and would therefore be attacked with a belt or a bat or a bar. He was constantly mocked and made fun of because of his disfigured and scarred skin. The McGuire's couldn't figure out why he was a target. He never said a word. He never did anything wrong. One day, Butchie McGuire asked an adult why they picked on this kid so much. Butchie was immediately beaten without warning and sent to a segregated cell. A few days later he was released and told his brothers about what these fucks did to him.

Two weeks later, while in the cafeteria, they saw one of the staff moving on the kid with a belt and for the first time, they heard his voice. But it wasn't a spoken word, it was a cry. The patient was hit two or three times when Butchie snapped, jumping on the staff member's back. That's all the McGuire boys needed to see. They weren't gonna let Butch be beaten again without getting their own licks in. And the fight was on. Other patients jumped in and that asshole was beaten from one end of the cafeteria to the other. Left with a massive concussion, this rat fuck couldn't remember anything. By the time the other staff arrived, they assumed it could have only been done by one patient due to his size alone, the poor kid that they continually targeted. As they surrounded him, one by one the McGuire kids spoke out, saying that they, and only they, had attacked him due to the attack on Butchie a few weeks earlier. As the McGuire boys were being escorted out of the cafeteria to an awful torture session that awaited, they saw the boy smile for the first time. That boy was Danny.

From that point on, they couldn't get rid of Danny if they tried. He was attached to their hips no matter what. They would learn that Danny was targeted mostly because he refused to participate in the fighting matches with other patients that were arranged by the staff. Danny knew he was bigger than most of the staff members and knew he would destroy any kid he faced. He would rather take a million beatings than hit some defenseless kid for no reason. But no-one ever stood up for him before.

Naturally this hell-hole bred an 'every kid for himself philosophy', and for the most part, that stood with everyone except the McGuire's. None of the other kids would even attempt to attack or steal or take advantage of them with Danny by their side. Soon the McGuire clan would learn how to pick locks. They would break into staff offices and lockers after hours. They would steal food and cigarettes and sometimes even booze. They would disperse all they stole to all in their ward evenly. They would only demand silence and allegiance and intelligence. Not brain intelligence but information on staff and their movements and comments. Who is doing what? Who is going on vacation? They became the de-facto Mayors of the joint.

Some staff members were worse than others and the kids prayed that they were going on days off, the boys' learning the staff's work patterns. Soon, the McGuire boys began making trips to the dark room. This was usually done after hours when everyone was asleep. A few months later, Danny would begin to notice spots of blood on the back of his friend's pants.

Woodhaven would eventually be shut down due to serious pressure from media and politicians. Advances were being made in the care for the legitimately handicapped. And a nationwide trend saw the closings of such places within the next 10 or 20 years. The biggest reason Woodhaven closed years before the others were because of three murders which took place on a single night.

You would hear horror stories years later on how unreported murders were committed there more often than most could imagine. But this night was different. These murders would be reported. Because the three victims were staff members. All three had their throats slashed and no less than 100 stab wounds. All three were males with their penises removed and with their respective murder weapons being forced up their rectums. All dead in the same ward. All were questioned at length including Danny and the McGuires. None said a word. All saw nothing.

The publicity and shame were too much for the state to bear. Especially as the media was stepping up its game with deeper and more detailed reports on the shithole, the place was shut down. The murders were never solved. Boo fucking hoo.

15

Party at Club Butch

Every year Butchie McGuire hosts a family gathering. It's held at his house because as a former firefighter, naturally he is the richest of the siblings. Gorgeous house. Sprawling backyard. Pool. Games. And the food and drink is endless. Beer by the keg or bottle and none of it will go to waste. Lobsters, steaks et al. The party usually starts in the morning and ends the following morning.

Butch is a portly white man with a totally legit afro and thick mustache. He resembles the Pringles guy. And he could polish off a 30 pack of beer during lunch alone.

Everyone is there. The siblings, their children, and their grandchildren. And of course, Uncle Danny. It's usually the best day of the year. The day you can't wait for and surely can't miss. Better than Christmas.

Jason is there, but he hardly knows one day from the next. It's been over a year since he was indicted for two counts of felony assault. Nothing seems to make sense. He is in an unforgiving

spell of depression. And anger. Some of it PTSD
related. Some of is diagnosed as post- concussion syndrome. He took a good beating that night
and still can't remember most of it. That's the
hardest part. The memory. What happened and
how it happened. His accusers' left Inspector Bucci's office that night with one story. Completely
synced....

They were standing on the street corner deciding what to do next. Wishing each other a Merry
Christmas. They were reveling in the time of year
when all is good and calm under the Lord. Nothing but happy thoughts. When out of the shadows
appeared this mean old Scrooge. He came at
them with a vengeance. He said nothing, but
pulled out a gun without provocation and began
pistol-whipping everyone in the group. Some fled.
But some were brave. Some stayed and tackled
this mad man to ground, disarming him, and saving humanity.

They all claimed that none were aware that he
was a cop. WHAT!!! This had to be bullshit. This
had to be a story fed to them by Bucci. But what if
it wasn't? That's why having no memory was the
hardest part. The unknown. What he did remember was the initial back and forth, the arguing.
Trying to get away. Being cornered. Identifying
himself. And reaching for his firearm. So it was

obvious that major portions of their stories were complete and utter bullshit. But the parts he couldn't remember, did he actually pistol whip someone? And why? Was it self-defense he thought. But he knows himself. He's trained for these moments his entire career. He knows what he would do and how he would think. And he knows he wouldn't pull his firearm unless he truly intended on using it. Definitely not to strike some-one with it. So why didn't he shoot? He surely couldn't hurt someone by striking them with it. It's an off duty piece. A .380. It's made of a poly plas-tic. It's a total piece of shit. It would shatter if he used it as a baton or striking device. Something wasn't adding up.

And all he did was think. And he had a lot of time. Nothing but time. Suspended without pay. Nowhere to stay. Nowhere he wanted to stay. He didn't want to be around others, including his fami-ly. He didn't trust what he would do or how he would act. The depression the head injury brought on was like no other. And the migraines. God aw-ful migraines. He spent days and months fighting bad urges. Horrible urges. Suicidal thoughts. Homicidal thoughts. Jason's brain was misfiring. And it couldn't be controlled.

At the time, most major sports had just begun paying attention to head trauma. But none truly were aware of its full effects. It was bad. He was walking dead. There physically and only physically. He couldn't remember one thought from the next. He was an awful son. An awful friend. An awful partner when he found a woman that could stand him for more than a few weeks or months. And he was an awful father. Inattentive. Quick tempered. And broke. Flat broke.

And he sat at this party. And he needed this party. Because if there was one thing he could never do, he could never bring the McGuire mood down. They were going to laugh and drink and drink and laugh. He may have seemed out of it, but he was all there, if only physically in Uncle Butch's backyard. On the inside, he was there, in the present. And it was therapeutic for him. To be around loved ones. To hear them curse and laugh and make fun of Feldman and Bucci. To hear Uncle Danny constantly babble "I'm gon' hurt them. You see". You don't want to fuck with Danny's family.

To be around his son, and watch him swim like a fish and play with other kids. That would bring Jason into another dimension. Like an out of body experience. Just floating on air. And happy.

Dennis would be there partying up a storm and soon becoming his drunken alter ego, Charlie. It was his split personality. From stoic and stone faced. To smiling and swearing and singing and dancing. Or at least attempting to dance. And forget it if anything from The Temptations would blast out of the speakers. That's when the party really started. With the McGuire brothers taking the stage and Dennis leading them. Jason loved Charlie. But the fun would only last a few moments. Then he was back to thinking. What did I do wrong? Who did I piss off? Are they setting me up?

He thought back to the most tragic day he ever experienced on the job, when a detective was murdered inside headquarters. The shots rang out and the mission began. Where is this motherfucker? Where is he hiding? The search was on. And during that search, Jason found the chief. Hiding behind a door. Their eyes connected. That look on his face, he'll never forget. Fear. The chief was frozen and couldn't move. Was that it? Was it because he saw him that night for what he truly was? Not a leader. But a complete pussy. Was he mad that Jason told anyone and everyone what he witnessed that night? He had no idea. What could it have been?

He was totally unaware of his father's dealings with Feldman. Unaware that he made Feldman piss his pants. Unaware of his role in the academy scandal. He blamed himself for everything. And as Dennis/Charlie drank and sang, he saw Jason sitting in a corner by himself. All day and night. Dennis was almost as tormented as his son. Because Dennis knew what this was about. Or at least had a feeling. And he too blamed himself for his son's current predicament. He never could have guessed it would happen though. You never fuck with another cop's kid. That's the rule. But Feldman wasn't a cop. He didn't know or care about any sacred unspoken rules on The Job.

Dennis tried keeping Jay occupied. He took him golfing constantly. Jason sucked and usually would lose all his golf balls within the first five holes. Dennis would carry extra and hand them to his son, telling him to cross off his ball marker so they didn't get confused. A marker is something placed on a golf ball with a permanent marker. It is in case you lose sight of the ball as it travels. Or if you hit a shot too close to someone else and you happen to be using the same brand. The marker is usually something unique to the ball's owner. Jay usually enjoyed guessing what his father's mark would be. It was usually numerical and related to the dates of birth of Dennis' grandchildren. He loved getting a ball with his own son's birth date on it. He thought it meant good luck. His golf game needed all the help it could get.

The Job

Jason was exhausted and wanted to leave hours earlier, but his son wanted to stay. He never got to do anything lately. There was no money. The least Jay could do was stay and let his son play till he dropped. He sat and watched as the night wore on.

Now people could barely stand. Except for him and Danny. Jason refused to drink and Danny was addicted to soda, leaving a trail of soda cans everywhere he went. They sat in a corner together and made fun of the party animals all night. Something about Uncle Danny always made him smile. A big baby-Huey brute of a man, but with the mind of a 6 year old. He told jokes like a child would. Innocent jokes. He'd stick his tongue out and thumb his nose. But he also held down a full time job as a janitor at RI Hospital. He loved it. He'd do it for free if they'd let him. He spent the rest of his time hanging with Jason's cousin Derek at the Broad St. Fire Station, the same house Uncle Butch worked at before calling it a career. He was the house's mascot. Their firehouse dalmatian.

And Danny had stories to tell. The man had been to hell and back and bought the t-shirt. But through it all, he always carried a positive message like a preacher would. So this had to get better right? This is small potatoes compared to what Danny went through. Jason would take a million indictments and suspensions to avoid that kind of upbringing. To be beaten over and over again. Who the fuck does that to anyone, never mind a child?

Danny would recite entire episodes of CSI and Forensic Files like he was reading from the script. He was the fucking Rain Man. And sometimes listening to his impromptu broadcasts would be better than watching the show itself. Actually, stabbing oneself in the eyeballs repeatedly with a thumbtack was better than watching that fake police show garbage.

Danny would continually ask "want me to take care of dat' for you". Jason would tell him no. That it was all set and he'd be alright. He knew what Danny meant. Danny was only trying to talk tough, he thought. But what the fuck good would that do? Throw the Chief a beating and get arrested? Danny would make the perfect patsy. And damn did it seem tempting. But you couldn't even joke like that with Danny. He didn't get sarcasm.

As time went on Jason bounced from doctor to doctor. He started having rage-induced black outs on a regular basis. No one really knew how to treat this shit. Mostly, he did nothing. Couldn't find work as a felon cop. He spent a lot of time with his son when he could. But mostly, he kept to himself.

He found comfort in music and football. Listening to 'Original of the Species' on a constant loop playing in his car with photos of his son all over the dash. And the Patriots, led by Tom Brady the almighty, always brought a smile to his face #fuckgoodell.

He had to constantly concentrate on his thoughts. He had to at least attempt to control them. He was full of anger. He wanted nothing more than to act on the anger. But he also knew that they didn't have him here. They had nothing. The worse thing he could do was fuck up now while awaiting trial or a resolution. Then they'd have him. And there'd be no coming back from that.

So he had to imagine and fantasize about the Chief being tortured. He had to imagine Bucci being dismembered, slowly. And the thoughts grew worse and more frequent. They were just about ready to take full control when Jason was referred to a doctor, a neuropsychologist. This doctor from RI had actually developed some of the testing and studies being used by leading experts in the field of head injuries. The doc, Frank, met with Jason once and within an hour, everything changed.

He explained to him why he was going through the constant changes. Especially the bad thoughts. He explained how the mind was processing and looking for new paths in order to rebuild itself. He explained that while he's having certain thoughts today, within the next two months the thoughts will begin to change to this or that. And he was right. Most importantly, because he knew not only what Jason was feeling, but what he was going to feel in the near future, he let him know that he was normal. That this is what happens with these types of injuries.

That helped Jason immensely. To know that he wasn't completely lost, and although he still had to fight because these urges still could take over, that he was normal. That slow roasting and carving of his enemies was a completely natural way to think under the circumstances. And that eventually, his memory would improve as well as his mood. This news helped a great deal. And it got him pumped. Pumped for his trial. Motivated for his redemption. And excited for the opportunity to embarrass the city. If only they'd stop stalling and bring it to trial already.

16

Another Dead Junkie

A car was dispatched to Paterson Park on the city's east side at about 2330 hours. The call was for fireworks violations. It had to be fireworks. Shots were not fired in this area of the city. These people were the elite and they let you know it. The police chief lived about 3 blocks away from the park in a home that no police chief in the world should be able to afford.

A patrol unit takes the call and arrives minutes later. Her spotlight is pointed towards the park and she can see a figure sitting on a park bench. She calls out but gets no response. Now she has to exit her vehicle and she is pissed. "Hey asshole, the park is closed" as she approaches. Still no response. As she gets closer, she can see it's a male. His skin is gray and he looks lifeless. He's wearing blue jeans and a grey sweatshirt. She doesn't see any apparent signs of trauma. Shining her light to the ground, she spots a firearm between his feet. She carefully circles around be-hind him and observes the back of his head is here, there, and everywhere. "Great, a fucking suicide" thinking of the paperwork. A supervisor and detectives are notified.

Upon examining the deceased a little closer, a frightening chill goes up her spine. It's Brandon Feldman, the Colonel's oldest. Another dead junkie. The scene is placed on lockdown as usual, but even more so this time. The Chief is notified and responds. Overwrought with painful grief, he can't stop grabbing and holding his son. The officers on scene want to tell him to stop, to preserve all evidence. But he's the fucking Chief. Who's gonna tell him? More bosses arrive and convince the Chief to respond home to be with his family. He knows his son feels no pain. No more urges. No more addictions.

The scene is processed slowly and thoroughly. There is not much evidence other than the firearm and a spent shell casing. A few soda and beer cans are in the immediate area as well as cigarette butts. Not much else. The east side parks are usually spotless. The city Department of Public Works sees to that. Fuck the rest of the city.

Looking at the deceased from the front, he appears to be fine. No signs that a bullet just ripped through his skull. He appeared to be peacefully sleeping. From behind, it looks like his head was pushed through a meat grinder. Like fresh hamburg.

The Job

The medical examiner arrives and begins his inspection. The pockets are searched. In one, an ID is pulled confirming what the cops already knew. In another, a folded paper is pulled. It is opened and examined briefly and appears to be typed and it is clear from the beginning that it is a suicide note. It's read no further and folded back and placed in an evidence bag to be turned over to BCI detectives.

A review of the body reveals an entrance wound in the upper roof of the mouth with exit naturally being the rear top of the head. Trauma and gasses macerate the brain as it exploded through the skull. Death was instantaneous. A grid is set up and all officers participate in a search for further evidence, attempting to find the projectile. Not that it matters. It's a clear suicide from a an extremely troubled kid.

All the east side cops dealt with him almost daily. They knew of his drama and alleged hatred for his father though it was clear to all that he didn't mind the beautiful house and the nonstop flow of cash his dad provided. Most thought he was just a spoiled east side junky.

The Chief returns to the scene as it's cleared. The Medical Examiner pulls off with the deceased. The Colonel is inconsolable. No one says a word.

They quietly snap their best salute to the chief and go back into service. The Chief inquires with detectives about any further evidence found, hoping this could have been an accidental shooting. No parent wants to accept the fact that their child committed suicide. The BCI Lieutenant, always looking to kiss ass, notifies the Chief about the note found. The Chief demands to read it and the Lieutenant puts up no resistance, handing it over to him.

He reads about how difficult Brandon's life was in the shadow of his "hero dad". The note takes a dark turn though, explaining that dad is no hero. The note tells of tales of mental and sexual abuse that lasted for years at the hands of his father. It states that it is clear that his father adopted him simply to satisfy his sick sexual urges. It states that recently, he discovered that his dad was being sexually abusive to his other children and this angered him to no end. Not because they were victims, but because in some sick, twisted way, he fell in love with his father and thought what they shared was unique to them. Like somehow, his father was cheating on him. He apologized for having to do things this way. But he knew that if he reported the abuse, specifically to Metro PD, he'd be brushed aside. No one took him seriously and they would assume he was lying and acting out. But doing it this way, he would ensure that authorities would take him seriously. And that his monster of a father would be stopped once and for all. It ended with an ominous message "Prepare for the sons a place of slaughter because of the iniquities of their fathers. Isaiah 14:21".

The Chief has seen enough. He tears the paper to shreds to the point it couldn't be repaired, screaming out "you fucking bastard". He knows it's not true. Not a word of it. But he doesn't care that this is valuable evidence, only about his reputation. He's no longer crying. He's fucking angry. Narcissistic asshole. No one will ever know the contents of the note. The detectives that still remain on scene look on stunned. *"What the fuck is he doing? What was in that note?"* But what do you say to the man? He's your chief and all had come to learn that no rules apply to this guy. The narcissist in him took over.

Citing Jewish tradition regarding certain death practices, he ordered that no autopsy be performed and he had his son's remains immediately shipped back to New York for burial. The bright side to his whole ordeal for the Chief was that he wouldn't be available for McGuire's trial which was to start the next day.

17

The Trial

The date of trial was finally here. It had been a long time coming, consistently being postponed by the city. They were hoping McGuire would settle and accept a deal. Or go off the deep end, allowing them to terminate his employment for good. Or worse, put a bullet through his own head. The city, especially the Chief, didn't care. Sure they would have mourned him publicly and all the bullshit that went with that, *troubled cop, lost his way, blah blah blah.* But they would have accepted that kind of victory.

They were lined up in the hallway as McGuire was pacing back and forth. He had a million questions. None of them for the witnesses. His only questions were for Bucci and the Chief. The Chief was out officially on bereavement, but McGuire's attorney was going to push the judge to issue a subpoena for him, but they didn't need him to crush the city.

McGuire's attorney, Kevin Bristow, was standing in a conference room, whispering his opening arguments to himself. Bristow is a true beast of a man. A cross between a great white shark and a

Peterbilt Truck. Massive and mean. Then, cue
the Imperial March theme, Bucci emerges from
around the corner, walking towards the courtroom.
He's wearing his best suit, black on black, like he's
attending a funeral. Bucci looks like he's dropped
40 pounds from his already tooth-pickish frame
since McGuire last saw him. He stops to greet
McGuire. McGuire laughs in his face and lets
Bucci know that he would be out of a job by the
end of this trial. He continues down the hall and
stops to greet McGuire's father, the retired Major.
Popping a salute, hand shaking uncontrollably,
Bucci greets him "Major". Dennis McGuire places
his hands in his pockets, looks down to the floor,
and simply states "not today, Sergio". Bucci continues into the courtroom and meets with the prosecutors assigned to the case. A decent, hard-
nosed veteran and a snotty incompetent rookie
are representing the state. McGuire can hear his
father and the court sheriff laughing, the sheriff
stating "did he actually just try to say hi to you"? A
few minutes later, Bucci leaves the courtroom,
walking around the corner, never to be seen
again.

*I could follow him right now. Maybe he'll turn
into a bathroom and I could drive an icepick
through his brain stem. No one would ever know.*

The prosecutors then exit the room and ask for defense attorney Bristow. They enter the conference room and within seconds, Bristow can be heard screaming. Chairs can be heard slamming to the floor, desks are being moved, all assumedly by Bristow, an animal by trade. This guy had a reputation for being a psycho. Just the kind of lawyer McGuire wanted. Bristow bursts from the conference room demanding to see McGuire and his father. As they enter, Bristow rips into Dennis.

Bristow: "What the fuck did you just say to Bucci?"
Dennis: "Nothing" Dennis replies.
Bristow: "Bullshit" Bristow screams.

Dennis moves towards Bristow rapidly, Jason getting between the two.

Dennis: "He tried to shake my hand, you cocksucker. All I said was not today, Sergio'".

Bristow let them know that Bucci just approached the prosecutors and told them that Dennis had threatened to kill him, at which time the prosecutors brought him into the Judge's chambers. The Judge was ordering that Dennis not be allowed in the courtroom either to testify or as an onlooker. Dennis runs out to the hallway and grabs the Sheriff. The Sheriff explains to both

Bristow and then the Judge that Bucci was lying about the exchange, that no such threats were made. But the tone was set. Bucci demanded that prosecutors take him off the witness list, that he refused to take the stand.

This is what angered Bristow the most. This had never been done before in RI criminal trials. Never has the investigating and arresting officer not taken the stand, in a case that he put together, by his own request. In fact, as the case agent, the investigating officer is supposed to be present in the courtroom, sitting beside the prosecutor for the duration of the trial. He refused to even enter the courtroom. With five minutes before opening arguments, Bristow is being told that he has to update the state's witness list. Bucci was shitting his pants. And he knew what was coming.

He knew that McGuire had the entire case folder regarding his very own off-duty incident in which he shot a guy half his size. 5 feet 4 inches and 130 pounds to be exact. Not 1 onto 15 as in McGuire's case. 1 on 1. Against a guy the size of a child. And why? Because he thought the guy was hitting on his wife. It was all right there in the file. In black and white. This other agency bent over backwards to help him, allowing him to change his own witness statement 3 or 4 times. He knew he would face questions about his past in the drug trade. His past in the narcotics bureau where he was ripping off drug dealers, taking their product and money on behalf of his family. How he would use his badge to muscle dealers off certain corners in order for his own relatives to work the locations.

He was going to be asked why he showed the douchebags in this case a single photo of the detective. Standard practice is to show a photo pack, or when it involves a cop, the department photo log and have them flip through the book of hundreds of officers. Not simply to hold up a single photo and go "this is the cop, right?" Or instead of asking the douchebags to describe the firearm, why would he show them the gun and say "this is the gun, right"? It was clear that he led these witnesses and directed the narrative. Why? What would he have to gain? What did the Chief tell him over the phone on the night of the incident? Was it the Major's position he was promoted to? From sergeant to Major no less, completely skipping Lieutenant and Captain.

Who knows why, but now he's running scared. But the stupid fuck obviously doesn't know how trials work. The prosecutor doesn't have to call him to the stand. The defense can. As Bristow stated in his opening arguments, when he dramatically walked over to the courtroom door in true Law and

The Job

Order fashion and yelled out "I hope you can hear me Sergio, because if the state doesn't call you, we will!!"

Bristow told the court he would prove 3 simple things. 1) None of these events ever happened as stated. McGuire never removed his firearm and pistol whipped anyone.
2) If he did remove his firearm and strike someone, it would be proven that it was in complete self-defense AND that McGuire would have been justified using deadly force. 3) That this was a bias and vendetta based investigation directed by the Chief, stemming from a poor history between the Chief and McGuire's father.

Bristow: "And to prove it your honor, we find out 5 minutes before opening arguments that the lead investigator, the arresting officer refuses to take the stand!!"

That spoke volumes. The Judge didn't let on that he was affected by this, but how could anyone not take notice of this?

The state presented its first witness, douchebag #1. By the time he was finished with the cross examination, he was crying. What a shit show. Funny as hell. Most notable was that now, all of a sudden, he didn't remember seeing a gun or anyone getting struck with a gun. But he knew a gun was there because douchebag #2 said he saw it.

Douchebag #2 takes the stand and it gets even worse. This kid has the brain of a raisin. Sees nothing. Knows nothing. Remembers nothing, except for one thing. He definitely didn't see a gun. No way. The way he explained it, douchebag #3 saw the gun.

Douchebag #3 takes the stand. Now shit gets real. He explains that douchebag #1 is doing most of the talking with the detective, and he can sense that it's escalating. So he "flanks" McGuire. This fuckhead actually uses the term "flank" on the stand. He was never in the military, but obviously played Call of Duty in between sessions of banging his own hand. And when he sees him bend down and reach towards his ankle, he "roundhouse" kicks the detective in the back of the head, a technique he learned through several years of "MMA training". He stated that he then "picked him up in the air, turned him upside down, and drove him head first into the ground". McGuire, sitting at the defense table thinks "well there's the concussion". But then douchebag #3 kicks it up a notch. "Then I grabbed his head and slammed it 3 or 4 times into the curb". He was asked was it the pavement or the sidewalk. He responds "no. the sharp edge of the granite curbing". This is the first McGuire has ever heard this account. Shocked, he looks towards the gallery, and he can see the horror on his father's face as well as other onlookers. *"What the fuck just happened?" he thought, "this fucking kid tried to kill me?"* Overcome with emotion, McGuire fought back tears and could only think about his son. Realizing the full extent of the trauma caused and the absolute possibility that this could have ended much worse, felt like being assaulted all over again. *"And my job put me on trial?"* he thought. He could have died. And his son could be fatherless. All because of some drunken fucking loser asshole that had left the stand earlier in tears. McGuire saw red, and it took every last fiber in his body to stop him from jumping into the witness box and killing this piece of shit. Or running out of the room to find Bucci. And douchebag #3 wasn't done. After slamming McGuire's head into the curbing, he then "rolled him over and punched him in the face 3 or 4 times".

At this point in the testimony, McGuire is verging on a blackout, and almost doesn't hear douchebag #3 state "oh I never saw a gun, douchebag #1 mentioned a gun".

Douchebag #4 for the state takes the stand and adds bits of stories taken from the first 3 and proceeds to get beaten into submission by the defense.

The state then actually has the balls to put officers that responded to the scene that night on the stand. Officers that heard these fucks say they knew McGuire was a cop as they were attacking him, although Bucci had coached them to say that they weren't aware until after the event.

Cop after cop, including bosses took the stand and all destroyed the state's case even though they were the state's witnesses. At a few points, the Judge stopped to ask the prosecutors "did you interview this witness"? They had nothing for the state. Nothing that could help the city. This went on for a week. All McGuire could do was fantasize about Bucci and Feldman. These motherfuckers were going to jail after this, never mind losing their jobs.

The state rested their case at end of the first week at which time the defense asked the Judge to dismiss all charges prior to calling its first witness. Known as summary judgement, it is common practice for defense attorneys to ask for a dismissal as soon as the state rests it's case claiming that the state hasn't proven guilt beyond a reasonable doubt up to that point. It happens in every case. Getting the dismissal is almost impossible though. The threshold the Judge has to use is extremely tough to jump over. Especially if the defendant is a cop in a blue state. No Judge wants to be known as favoring a cop. What would the public think? "The fix is in!" The Judge takes the dismissal under advisement and tells Bristow to have the first defense witness ready for Monday morning.

The longest weekend in the history of weekends is upon us. McGuire can't eat or sleep. His stomach is in knots, his migraines kick into high gear. One more weekend to survive. One more weekend to keep it all together. Just one more weekend to keep both feet on the ledge, *"don't jump"*. What witness would they call first? Should they call any witnesses except Bucci? Please, please, please, let's call him first. *Or wouldn't it be easier to just go to his house and take out that cocksucker right now.* After hearing that week of testimony, it's clear to McGuire that Bucci and Feldman wouldn't have lost a minute of sleep if he had died.

Fuck them. They don't deserve to live. No. No. Hold it together. You can get them back some other day. One more weekend and you can at least revel in the looks on their faces when you win. Then kill them. Yeah that's it. Wait, once you win, it's you and your son living without this hell

*hanging over the two of you. It's peace. Finally.
Ok, don't kill anyone. Show them you're not affected at all. Smile. That would really fuck with
them.*

What to do? What to do?

Monday morning, 9 AM. It's time for the fireworks that Bristow had promised in his opening argument. It was time to put the city on trial. But
first the Judge had to rule on the motion to
dismiss. Reading from notes, the Judge begins
addressing the court to his findings. It lasts forever. But several minutes in, Bristow can sense
where it is going. The Judge had done nothing but
bash the state's case up to this point. He grabs
McGuire's hand under the table and whispers "I
think we won". McGuire is in a fog. He's trying to
follow the Judge's statements, some of which
seem to blame him. He has to blame the detective a little. This way it doesn't look like he's favoring him simply because he's a cop. But he's making it clear that McGuire should not be in his courtroom sitting at the defense table. It's clear to the
court that McGuire is the victim. Confused, he
looks over to his father who is smiling and Dennis
gives him "the wink".

The Judge explains that he has a sense where
this trial is headed, to the top, and he doesn't want

to see where it ends up. And just like that, the case is over. Acquitted of all charges.

McGuire sits there, still in a fog. He truly doesn't understand what the fuck is going on. His attorney is breaking into a half dance. His family is in the gallery smiling and crying at the same time. One of the prosecutors reaches down and extends his hand and whispers "this was bullshit from the beginning. Sorry. Just following orders". That's when it hits him. This is over. *This is fucking over!!* He tries to chase the Judge down to beg that the case continue, but he's already disappeared. People are extending their hands but he can't. He smacks them away.

Bristow: "We won"
McGuire: "We won what Kevin?" "What the fuck did we win?"

This wasn't about winning the case for McGuire. He knew he was going to win. That was the easy part. For him it was about Bucci. It was about the Colonel. That was his justice. He wanted them on the stand. And now they've escaped. There was no justice in this. McGuire was angrier than he had ever been, to that point. He saw red. Blood red. He'd have to get his justice a different way.

18

The Road Back

Some time had passed and McGuire was doing everything he could to get back to living semi-normally. He found a nice condo he planned on turning into ass central. Prior to that, a close friend had tried to help him get on his feet, inviting him to join in one of his many restaurant ventures. Having nothing better to do, Jay took him up on the offer and into the dreadful restaurant business he went. It was a total disaster. As if opening a small take-out spot in the middle of a recession wasn't bad enough, not having liquor license was worse. At least in a recession, liquor sales don't decrease, in fact they increase. But he tried his hardest and plugged away. It was truly the hardest thing that he had ever done. The hours were never-ending. The food orders were constant. At the end of every good day in sales, he would learn that a million more items needed to be ordered for the next morning. There was never a penny to be made. Restaurant owners around the world truly need to have their heads examined. McGuire gave it his all, but ultimately decided that it was 10 times harder than walking into a crime scene that is covered in brain matter.

The Job

As soon as the trial ended, regular pay checks from the department began coming in again, although he was still out of work, not having been cleared for a full return. So he sat around. He set up his new place nicely. And especially went overboard in his son's bedroom feeling the need to overcompensate for the recent down times. All that was needed now was an endless flow of ass. But in actuality, he didn't have the energy to go out and look. So Xbox and vegging out was all he did.

One night, he decided to go out for a later than usual dinner of the almighty fast food. While passing a friend and neighbor in the hallway, he saw that he and his wife were carrying a bag of the best smelling food in the history of food. They told him how they had just found a small Chinese restaurant around the corner and that he had to try it. Jay exited the property and took the long way to the local strip of fast food heaven, making sure to at least inspect the Chinese restaurant. As he passed, it looked empty and closed. He pulled around back and quickly realized that the customers all had chosen to park in the rear lot. He goes in and is told to make a take-out order at the bar which he approaches. He's immediately taken aback by this beautiful creature sitting at the bar. Stunning would be an understatement. To Jay, it seems like she might be spoken for though as she is sitting next to a much older gentleman. He thinks to himself that she is definitely a trophy girl-friend, that this guy must have serious coin, a sugar daddy. The pervert in Jay thinks high-end prostitute, definitely. He orders his food and before he knows, the old man is making conversation with him, recognizing McGuire from a past dealing. He introduces Jay to the goddess sitting to his right and introduces her....Renee. McGuire was shocked, totally expecting a stripper's name like Amber Lynn or Summer Storm. But it's clear after only a few minutes that they are not together, just friendly and sitting next to each other at what is the smallest, tightest squeezing bar in the world.

That is all McGuire needed. It was time to see if he still had the old mojo in him. Certainly not looking his best, he reaches deep into his bag of tricks, pulling out his true magic, his gift of gab. McGuire has been known to talk to a telephone for 3 hours and actually have a meaningful conversation. And he goes for the fences with this one thinking fuck it, if he strikes out, he'll more than likely never come back to this joint anyway. 3 hours later, they depart having exchanged numbers and after deciding when was the best time to meet up at the same spot.

Jay goes home, thinking positively and confident. Confident that it's time that he gets back out there laying the traps for the womenfolk. He truly felt that he was given a wrong number and that Renee was just a mirage, a cruel joke from God. But ah-ha, she reaches out to him within a few days. They talk for a few weeks and the first date is set, soon to be followed by several others. He's hooked beyond hooked and falls deep.

Renee soon see's McGuire's darker side. His torment, and his inability to make a decision on his future. She pushes him hard. She can tell that The Job is still a part of him and that he would never be truly happy until he returned. She won't let him rest until he at least gives it a shot.

He had met his soulmate and she was a god-send. She stuck with him a lot longer than she should have, and she had the scars to prove it. Not physical of course. In some ways, she was just as fucked up with her own demons. She could be straight-up warped at times. But Jay dug it. She found Jason to be a twisted, tortured soul. And she wouldn't give up on him. She wouldn't let him quit. She carried him longer than he deserved. And she took his son in as her own. She changed everything his heart and mind ever thought about life. She showed him a love and support that he had never ever experienced. And because of this, when she was at her darkest, he couldn't leave her. He owed her for the life-changing love that she brought into his world. And for the love that she showed his son. It was a no-brainer that they would one day marry.

19

Back On The Job

It took Jason several months before he could return to work. Mostly to carry a firearm. In recent years, in light of all the events, he might have been a little too honest with his shrink about things he'd like to do to certain people. He had to do a lot of lying and bullshitting in order to get his doctor to sign off on a return to full duty. He couldn't wait. He missed the job. He loved what he did. Especially being a detective. While his father had climbed the ranks, Jason never had it in him. If they thought his dad was strict, they'd fucking hate him for sure. All he wanted from the moment he graduated the academy was to become a major crimes detective. To start working homicides. Too much Andy Sipowicz on the brain and by now he had the belly to go with it. And it took no time to get back into the swing of things.

Right out of the gates he was catching murder cases left and right. And he was closing them out, all of them. He felt invigorated. He kept to himself and avoided the Chief like the plague. They'd naturally see each other in passing. It was inevitable. In fact, on his first day back the Chief made it into the squad room and welcomed him back in front of the whole bureau. He actually had the balls to say he was pulling for him the whole time. You could hear people whispering "bullshit" under their breath. But Jason wouldn't take the bait.

His philosophy was simple: he took the job for a reason, to help people and because of the "Bo Duke Affair". And those reasons still applied today. He knew that if he kept his head down and turned in great work, that would piss off the administration to no end. They wanted him to be a malcontent. They wanted him to be miserable and divisive. That's how The Job is. Many a good cop has been soured by his own department over the years, turning them into nothing but an empty suit for the remainder of their careers. The job had tons of them. All sorts of cops thinking they were fucked one way or another.

And the gossip. The fucking gossip. The Job, no matter where in the country, is nothing short of a soap opera. And the others tried hard to get Jason going. He was now working for the Lieutenant that couldn't make the right command decision on the night of his off duty incident. Jason didn't mind though. And he refused to take the bait. He actually enjoyed working for his Lieutenant.

It took a while, but after enough time passed, the guys realized he wasn't about to lead some holy war against the city. And maybe they learned a little something from it. He seemed to find ease closing big cases or identifying the bad guy. It was tough though. His brain was still misfiring. Where the good detectives are slow and methodical in their approach, Jason couldn't keep any less than 20 thoughts in his head at any given moment. He was all over the place. Although, that may have helped him. He had a weird imagination about things now and applied some unorthodox approaches to his work. He was able to look at things and angles where other detectives would say he was wasting his time. Some dead-ended. But some actually led to the jackpot, the smoking gun.

He learned how to put his bent mind to good use. Sometimes, thinking like, and getting into the minds of his suspects. Gone was his Rain Man like memory, one of his greatest assets. He couldn't remember shit now unless he wrote it down or had an audio recording. And the migraines were still there. Fast and furious. He used a lot of sick time. A ton actually. He never had a headache in his life prior to getting his ass kicked that night. Now he would find himself in a fetal position on the floor of a cold dark room for two, three days at a time.

He thought about quitting. But he was on a roll.

And the satisfaction he got out of closing a case was well worth the agony. It didn't matter if it was a petty crime. Work was a grind but now it was fun again.

They had just come off the best Christmas ever as a family. Everything seemed back to normal. Until right after New Year's Day. It started off like every other day in the winter. Work was slow. He was just finishing up his coffee and thinking about where he would park and light up a cigar while doing his paperwork. His sergeant called and asked him to respond up to City Park and help handle this bozo that wandered into the polar bear exhibit. He responded and the day's events would haunt him for a long time.

20

A Dirty Cop

The department is reeling. The deaths of a father and son on the job was unheard of. The Bucci matriarch had one request: Jason McGuire was not welcome to join the services. She and her family blamed him. Not for the death of Sergio Jr. But for the death of his father.

In recent years the Major was out of sorts. He knew he had skeletons and feared that they would be revealed one day. The gossip around the department was that McGuire was going to sue civilly or pen a tell-all. He thought his life was on the fast track when he conned this new Chief into believing in his bullshit, or so he thought. The Chief wasn't dumb. Feldman did his homework. He knew Bucci had severely compromised ethics. Who better to put in charge of Internal Affairs. A minion that would do his bidding. This only made Bucci's paranoia worsen. How could he fuck cops for doing much less than he did?

Bucci was the definition of a truly corrupt cop. And there were several guys still on the job that had gotten on with him. They knew what he was about. But this thing with McGuire put him into a tailspin. By now everyone knew how he ducked out of the trial. Everyone knew that he coached those assholes into leaving statements against McGuire. Bucci would spend his entire shift locked in his office. He took his reward, his promotion to major, and hid.

And by now he had become a raging alcoholic. His days were filled with booze and pain meds. His nights were a steady diet of Ambien and vodka. Bucci was now useless as a boss as well as a father and husband. He wandered around in a constant dreamlike state, not being able to determine the real from the imagined. And he blamed McGuire and his father for this. As did his family. He didn't blame himself for playing a dangerous game. It was everyone else's fault.

Unbeknownst to the job, Bucci had confided suicidal thoughts to his wife constantly. And it finally happened. And it was McGuire's fault. At least that is what they felt. And McGuire couldn't go against their wishes. And it killed him to have them feel that way. Though others in Jason's family, including his father, seemed to express delight in their tragedy, Jason wasn't like that. Sure he fantasized about hurting Bucci himself. But it ended there, just as thoughts. And he felt for the major at that moment, on that day. He knew he would have done the same to himself had he heard his own son was in that bear pit.

He stopped by the Bucci's home on the morning of the wake services. He stood at the door
and explained to Mrs. Bucci that he was saddened
for her loss and respected her wishes to he remain
unseen. But he had to at least tell her. She
slammed the door in his face but he was relieved
nonetheless. He said what he had to say. The
service and funeral drew thousands of cops from
around New England and the country. Motorcycles, bagpipes, honor guards. Cops truly know
how to bury one of their own, or two in this case.
Jason was the only officer at headquarters that
day. All were attending the funeral except for the
patrol cops on the street. Outside agencies
stepped up and helped cover calls.

Jason went through some of the evidence
seized in the case and sent some out to the state
lab for testing only as a formality. He closed out
the report and went to have a smoke on the east
side by the water. Today it was a Debonaire Cigar
made by Phil Zanghi in the Dominican Republic.
Overlooking the water, some of his former darker
thoughts seemed to creep up on him. He felt like
the outsider again. The unwanted. Like he wasn't
part of the job. By now they were probably tap-
ping the kegs at some local tap, listening to the
bagpipes, honoring their dead. And he wasn't

there. This was HIS job. The Job he grew up in. The Job he loved. And he was once again all alone and the outsider, if only for one day. But it seemed like an eternity. It felt the same as the years he spent awaiting trial.

While day-dreaming, McGuire was awoken by a cracking sound directly outside of his vehicle. It happened again and again and he couldn't figure out what it was. The parking lot was empty except for a few seagulls. Then it dawned on him, every time he heard the cracking sound, a seagull would swoop down and devour something off of the ground. He realized that the birds were pulling mussels from the ocean during low tide at which point they would lift off about 20 or 30 feet in the air and drop them to the pavement. The shells would explode exposing the meat inside. Over and over again they continued to do this. McGuire was stunned. *How did they learn to pull this shit off.* He wondered how long it took them to figure this out. Must have been years, but not hundreds or thousands of years of evolution. Pavement wasn't in existence for that long. This creature with a brain the size of a pea had to learn this simply to adapt and survive. McGuire watched this act in amazement for hours. And he realized that adapting and surviving was what he had been doing up to that point and that now was no time to stop.

21

The Chief Just Won't Learn

The following day McGuire is called in to the Internal Affairs office. The Chief is there along with the city attorney. "What's this about" he asks. They ask him if he would like a union attorney present. He declines. *"What did I do now?"* he's thinking. They asked him about his whereabouts on the evening and into the morning of Bucci's death.

"Are you fucking kidding me?" he yells. "This was a fucking accident or a suicide".

The Chief chimes in "oh I'm sure you'd like us to believe that".

Jason bursts out of his chair "fuck you. Are you out of your fucking minds?"

He argues how in the hell could he or anyone have gotten Bucci from wherever, into the zoo, and into the bear exhibit without Bucci putting up a fight and calling for help.

"Are the autopsy results final?" he asks. "Do you have any proof that this was anything but a suicide?"

They concede that the results aren't finished, but still demand to know where he was. They even ask for his cellphone and permission to examine it.

"And you were the first one in the office when the Major died" says Feldman.

Having already been through this before, McGuire loses it. He tells them to go fuck themselves and refuses to answer any questions or give up his personal phone, only his work cell. He is relieved of his gun and badge and put on paid administrative leave for insubordination and refusal to cooperate. That evening, the headline reads "Detective Placed On Leave In Investigation". The story doesn't mention specifics, but "sources" say it involves the death of Bucci. There's even quotes from Mrs. Bucci hoping that justice is found for her family.

It's all bullshit. They know these are not murders. But Feldman is at it again, will McGuire pop? It's not about evidence or justice. The Chief hasn't learned his lesson. Narcissistic cocksucker. Weeks go by and McGuire gets a call from a fellow detective telling him that there is a letter on his desk from the Department of Health. *"What could that be?"* he thinks. He asks him to open it and read it over the phone. The letter reads that the syringe found in Bucci's vehicle had come back with a hit for his DNA. It reads that there were also traces of a substance found in the syringe that could not be identified. Jason jumps out of his chair and rushes to headquarters.

22

New Evidence

After retrieving the letter, Jason has to wait for the Department of Heath to open the following day. He's there the moment they open and speaks directly to the person that analyzed the evidence. "What could it be?" he asks. He's told that a test was run for several legal and illegal substances such as heroin and steroids but came back with no results. He is also told that they don't have the ability on sight to test for certain modern designer drugs and that it would have to be sent elsewhere for further testing.

This could be the big break he thought. The break that could clear him. Some sick-ass designer drug that had him acting like a fucktard could have done this easily. The problem is that sending the sample out for further testing would cost money and it needed the departments approval. He begs the other detective to have it sent out to the FBI lab on the hush. He's reluctant but Jason promises him that he would stand up and take the hit if the job found out.

By now, word had gotten around that McGuire was inquiring about Bucci's behavior in the time leading up to his death to include possible drug use. It was a touchy subject and not only from the administration, the job too. Why would he ask such things if not to smear the fallen?

Weeks go by and McGuire gets the call, though not the call he wanted. He's being ordered to return to the Internal Affairs office. He responds this time with his former attorney, Bristow. Bristow has no love for the job and this time he wants blood. McGuire is advised that he is now being brought up on departmental charges regarding the investigation. He's told that while suspended, he deliberately ordered lab testing on evidence from a closed case at a cost to the department. Department rules are clear that any officer on suspension, paid or not, is not to be involved in anything remotely relating to police work. In fact simply identifying oneself as a cop while suspended is grounds for termination.

McGuire sits and thinks of the other detective, *"the fuck ratted me out"*. But soon he learns the truth. The testing was completed but instead of the results being forwarded directly to McGuire, they were mailed to the BCI office. The same BCI office whose snake Lieutenant had pleasure in delivering the letter directly to the Chief. McGuire is done, he can take no more. Against the advice of counsel, he offers to resign right then and there.

He had dreamt his whole life of The Job. But it's clear now that it doesn't want him. As he awaits for them to prepare the paperwork, he asks if he could simply see the results.

Feldmand: "Oh I'm sure you'd like that" the Chief says. "You'd love to rub this poor family's face in it".
McGuire: "No Colonel, I'm not like you. I believe in the code. You never attack a family member for a beef you have with one individual". He continues "If you or Bucci were ever found dead due to suspicious circumstances, you'd be right to look at me. But not your family. That's where you and me differ."

Jason has long dreamt of the Colonel's demise at the end of an ice pick or worse. What does he care now? What does he have to lose? He's quitting anyway. Maybe he can piss the Chief off enough where he actually grows a pair of balls and asks the detective to step outside. That would be the cherry on top for McGuire. To slay Commodus in the arena in front of everyone. Or more realistically, to beat the ever-loving shit out of him in the rear parking lot.

The Chief gives in, letting McGuire know that this would be the last piece of police work he would ever do. D-tubocurarine. "What the fuck is that?" they all seem to say together. An IA sergeant puts it into a search engine on his computer. "It's a muscle relaxant. A paralyzing agent". D-tubocurarine, commonly known as curare is a strong muscle relaxant. Made famous by indigenous South American tribes centuries earlier for use in poison darts.

McGuire: "Curare?? Who the fuck would inject themselves with curare? And how would they get across a park being totally paralyzed?" McGuire asks.

Seizing the moment, Bristow chimes in…

Bristow: "what did you get back from my client's cell phone? Where was it located that night?"
IA Sergeant: "At his house" the sergeant replies.
Feldman: "What does that matter?" Feldman jumps in. "He could have easily left it there to disguise his whereabouts".

The sergeant, finally having heard enough, speaks up:

IA Sergeant: "Chief, we have nothing here. We all know it. How can we hurt the kid when it's clear that he was on to something?"

Feldman: "On to what?" the chief yells out.

IA Sergeant: "The tests results" shoots back the sergeant, "there's something totally wrong with the Bucci scenario and he's obviously found something. Now if you want to fuck the kid, be my guest. You had your crack at him once and failed. I'm not going to be a part of this".

They disappear into the Sergeants office for a good hour. It's hard to tell whats being said, but it's clear that no one is being polite. And Jason knows that the Sergeant is loyal to his father. Eventually the Chief emerges and storms past McGuire and Bristow without saying a word. The Sergeant emerges shortly after and tosses McGuire's paperwork into the trash. He hands him his shield and firearm with a strict warning,

IA Sergeant: "From the Chief, and on behalf of the Bucci family, you're done with this case. Let someone else run with it".

McGuire: "You got it" McGuire replies, not truly planning on following the order. "Thanks Sarge".

He should, by right, head home for the day, or maybe even a week. He's earned it. Instead, he walks directly to the squad room where he learns the file has already been passed to some lazy nitwit, Frank Ventura. McGuire tells him he can't get involved, but asks him to please come to him if

The Job

he needs any help.

23

Curare??

*Curare. What does it do? What are its side ef-
fects? Where the fuck would you even get some
ancient Indian poison dart shit anyway?*

McGuire goes deep, looking for information via
the internet, books, doctors, anywhere. He learns
that it is a strong acting paralyzing drug used by
tribes to hunt prey for food. It would completely
stop all muscle movement on anything they were
hunting and was harmless if ingested. An animal
paralyzed by curare would have no side effects to
anyone that would later prepare it and eat it.

He also learns that although paralyzed, those
poisoned by curare don't go completely numb.
Their voluntary muscle system is shut down. But
they are fully conscious and can feel pain.
McGuire still can't get the image of Bucci Jr's skull
or blood out of his head. He's thinking *"could he
actually have been alive and felt the attack?
That he knew what was coming and could feel
every last bite up until death either by shock or
bleeding out?"*

He consults with a local anesthesiologist he

knew from the cigar lounge and learns that some hospitals may still keep it on hand. It's very effective, although modern science has found products with fewer side effects. But one thing is made clear, curare, like all paralyzing agents, will also stop the lungs after several minutes. It's normally used to calm the muscles in the throat in order to insert a breathing device during surgery. But without carefully administering the dose, and without a breathing device, a subject could eventually die.

It's clear to McGuire now that Bucci didn't use this on his own. Maybe another party goer or friend gave it to him believing it to be something else. Still, the syringe would have been near the bear pit, not in his vehicle. But how did someone hit him with this substance and still keep him alive long enough to get him across the park?

At the squad room, he grabs the case folder off of Ventura's desk. Naturally, it's under a pile of shit never to be worked on. He pours over his original notes looking for anything that would help him make sense of this. He can't find anything. He pulls the BCI photos of the scene both at the car and in the zoo and can't seem to locate anything he may have missed.

After several exhausting days, he decides to start back at square one, at the beginning. He responds back to the house where Bucci's car was found. McGuire walks from the car location along the most direct route to the entrance of the zoo and the bear exhibit. Nothing. He goes back and takes a different, more indirect route. Nothing. 3 attempts later, with what feels like 10 miles accumulated, he decides to call it a day. Before leaving the park, he stops in to see if Bob, the keeper, was around.

Bob: "Hey detective. Hopefully you're here on a better mission this time".

McGuire: "Nope" McGuire responds, "still working the first one".

He asks Bob if he had found or seen anything since that day that may have stood out to him.

Bob: "I haven't. Actually, a few days later we found that a chain on the rear service entrance gate to the park was cut with some kind of tool We didn't know if it was related but it is directly behind the bear pen. Other than that, only that respirator thing from that day".

McGuire's eyes pop out of his head. *RESPI-RATOR.*

McGuire: "The fucking respirator. Tell me you still have it".

Bob: "It should be back in the maintenance shed where I put it unless someone took it out" Bob says.

They hop in a golf cart-looking thing and rush over to the rear of the exhibit. Upon unlocking the door, there it is, in all its glory. McGuire's eyes are playing tricks on him. He swears he can see a bright glow coming from behind it as if sent by the heavens. Church bells are ringing in his head. He immediately radios for a BCI unit to respond and seize it. Before he can make it back to the station, he almost collapses. The stress. The excitement. He can feel his head building with pressure. He vomits violently. Zoo personnel get him a chair. He doesn't want one. All he needs is help getting back to his car which they help him with. As soon as he enters, he stabs himself in the thigh with a preloaded dose of the happy stuff and reclines his seat. Half awake, or more like half alive, he enters this dreamlike state.

24

A Vision

I've planned this for months. Following Bucci.
Figuring out his routine. I see him every night,
usually switching up his bar location. But I still
have to wait till Bucci decides to return home. A
few times, I thought I had him, but realized Bucci
wasn't drunk enough or was still too alert. But this
day was different. I followed him earlier that day
and saw that he was heading to Newport with
friends, more than likely to get hammered. Bucci
would be awake and drinking far too long to not be
feeling it when he got home. All I need is a
minute's time.

And tonights the night. It has to be. The car's
lights are off, window is down. I can hear the heat
blasting as I approach. Bucci would never hear
me. I quickly but carefully jab him in the shoulder
and duck behind the car. Bucci doesn't flinch. I
wait a minute or two and come up on him. Looking through the window, it's apparent the drug has
begun to take effect. His breathing is heavy. It's
now or never. Holding a firearm in my right hand
in case the plan changes, I nudge Bucci slightly
with my left. Bucci wakes. He can't move, can't
turn his head. He can see though, eyes wide

open.

*I secure the respirator to his face and around
the back of his head. I then run back to the other
side of the street to retrieve my own vehicle. I
load Bucci and make my way towards the park's
rear employee entrance. I snip the gate chain
with bolt cutters. No alarms ring out. I open the
back gate, leading directly into the park. The
coast is clear. I grab Bucci and drag him over to
the golf cart. The keys are in the ignition. It's winter and no one has access to the park except zoo
staff and veterinarians so there is no need to secure the keys. I make the trek with Bucci in tow all
the way to the bear exhibit. I drag him over one
railing and towards an inner fence.*

*Fire in my eyes, I get him just about over the
second fence when I rip off the breathing device. I
drop him, carefully sending him feet first. A head-
first fall would probably kill him. But I want him
alive long enough to feel it. I then run around the
back employee trail leading to the area adjacent to
the bear den. I bang and hoot and holler until the
bears emerge. Filled with ecstasy, I fly back over
to the railing, dropping the respirator in my haste.
Drawing the attention of the bears to the wall, I
watch as they first begin to inspect Bucci. They
smack him around a little. And then big mama
goes right for the throat. He's still alive, I can tell,*

*as blood shoots across the adult bear's chest.
And I'm euphoric to the point of sexual bliss. Bucci can't scream. He can't move. But he feels it.
And he knows it. He is probably wishing that this
is all a bad dream. And he wonders why he can't
wake from it. At some point, I don't know if he's
still alive or dead but it's obvious he ain't gonna
survive. My bloodlust satisfied, I make my way
back to the gate and off I go. My job is done. Revenge is mine.*

McGuire comes out of his stupor and is out of
sorts. He doesn't know where he is and can't remember how he got there. And he's frightened.
Frightened of his thoughts. Praying that he did
nothing wrong. And he rushes back to headquarters.

25

This Ain't Hollywood

Back at the station, he responds to his sergeants office with the news. "Sarge, I know I'm gonna get fucked for this, but hear me out". He explains what he has found thus far. The paralyzing poison. The needle with Bucci's DNA. The respirator found by a park employee that day and placed in the shed, never to be claimed by another employee. "I'm lost" Detective Sergeant Collins says. McGuire explains that Bucci could not have taken the curare himself. He was probably passed out drunk in his car. Someone pricks him with this shit in the arm or shoulder or neck, wherever. Within seconds, they wake him up and he realizes that he can't move or talk. He's stripped naked. They somehow get him in to the park, probably by vehicle or maybe stealing the cart. They keep him alive with this breathing device before they lower him into the pit. They wanted him to be eaten alive, to feel his last moments in pain and fear.

Collins wants to say good work, but this is some made for TV type shit. He tells the detective that he's "fucking crazy" and warns him to pass the info on and leave it alone. He passes it off as the detective and his brain damage maybe mixed

with booze. "You're reaching kid. He killed himself". McGuire walks down to the BCI office on the
first floor. The breathing unit has already been
dusted and swabbed. No prints were lifted. He
examines it. It looks old and worn. He observes
the marking "R4" on the side of it. He brings it
down the hall to the fire headquarters which is located in the same building as police. He shows it
to the local battalion chief who thinks it's one of
theirs, probably Rescue 4 which operates out of
the Broad St. fire house.

McGuire calls his cousin Derek and gets a coffee order for the station. Firefighters love free shit.
He shows it to the house Lieutenant who confirms
it's a spare unit of theirs and that it's been missing.

*Finally getting somewhere McGuire thinks.
Now, who the fuck am I looking at? Was Bucci
banging a fireman's wife? Wouldn't be the first
time. What about Bob? Not the movie. The zoo
employee. Or his partner. Who would have access to this device? And who could gain entry into
the park? A firefighter certainly could.*

But rescue apparatus are always left on scenes
with the doors open or unlocked as rescue personnel are assisting people in houses or motor vehi-
cles. Anyone really could have taken this respirator. He interviews all crew from the firehouse. He

calls in Bob and Maria from the park for another recorded statement. He seems to be so close, but he's hitting a wall. What is he missing? Motive is the key and he has none.

He knows the only thing to do is reach out to Mrs. Bucci. But he can't. The chief would surely have his head then. He asks Ventura to reach out. "What for, she wasn't there" Ventura states. "What do you mean what for? Anything we don't know right now. Ex-girlfriends. Ex-boyfriends. Problems with others. We have nothing right now to go with the evidence. The tiniest detail could open this up". "Yeah, yeah. Look, the kid fucked up, and got ate" says Ventura. *ATE!!* McGuire knows he can't trust him. And if he pushes him too much, he'll go to the bosses. Ventura's desk is where cases go to die.

26

Swerve To The Rescue

He reaches out to the only guy he can trust, his academy classmate and partner-in-smokes Kenny Court. Court, having no love for the current command structure in the detective bureau, happily agrees to help. And Court can talk. He's a smooth motherfucker. Acquiring the nickname "Swerve" years earlier. A nickname that to this date still hasn't been defined. But it sounds cool, almost pimp-ish. Lando Calrissian-esque.

Court is friendly with Major Bucci's daughter. He reaches out to her and explains that there have been a few unexplained developments in her brother's case. They agree to meet at which time she agrees to set up a meeting with Court and her mother. At the Bucci home, Court explains the effects of curare. Bucci Jr's toxicology hadn't come back yet from the lab which was expected. It's usually takes 3 to 6 months. But he asks if she knew of any other type of drug, specifically a designer party drug that he could have been using. This wasn't to smear the former patrolman, but more to understand the circumstances and to possibly move this from a suicide or accidental death, to a murder. But he also cautions her not to jump to conclusions.

Could he have been ingesting a party drug which acts like an "upper"? Combining it with curare as a "downer". Enough to keep him somewhat mobile, but maybe batshit crazy. Anything? Mrs. Bucci has nothing. She explains that when they cleaned out his apartment, she specifically looked for evidence of drug use or drinking. She looked for notes both written and on his computer to see if he kept a diary-type log. Anything that would indicate trouble or psychosis. She found nothing. He seemed to live as plain and quiet as a guy could. He was a single rookie patrolman. And he had a ton of luck with women. He didn't seem lonesome or depressed. A suicide definitely didn't seem possible. She never accepted that. In her heart, she thought that he probably wandered into the zoo while drunk for whatever reason and got too close to the railing. Maybe dropping his cellphone or something over the side and then attempting to retrieve it.

Not being around to ask him, Kenny asked her if Major Bucci would have considered this an accident. Did the Major have any concerns over his son's safety and mental well-being. The Major was a touchy subject for Mrs. Bucci. He had become nearly invisible before his death. Losing close to 70 pounds on a pure liquid diet. She said he spent every night and all weekends comatose. He spent no time with her or their children. He would thrash violently in his sleep. He'd toss and turn and sleepwalk and scream out gibberish and nonsense. In the overnight hours before the incident, she stated that she awoke to him mumbling into his phone. He did that often she explained. She hadn't heard it ring and thought he was in the middle of one of his dreams. She asked him who he was talking to and he repeated the phrase "sins or sons of the father" 2 or 3 times. He never opened his eyes and soon began snoring. He didn't remember the call when he woke up in the morning so she thought nothing of it.

Kenny asks to see the Major's personal cell phone and notes there was in fact an incoming call that morning at 0447. The caller ID indicated that it was made from her son's phone. *Interesting,* Court thought to himself. Maybe this was his suicide note. Maybe he was telling his father what he planned to do. Kenny asked if he could keep the phone. Then he explained to Mrs. Bucci that pending the results of toxicology, this may end up becoming an open investigation. He advised her not to get her hopes up, but he knew it would be much more comforting for her to know that this was not in fact a suicide or even an accident. She might have the chance to focus her thoughts on a single source. And dream of justice.

The Job

Before Kenny leaves, Mrs. Bucci has one question, why? "Why are you doing this? You didn't know my son. Why isn't the Chief or another member of the administration here?" Kenny reluctantly replies "I'm not doing this ma'am. Jason McGuire dug up this evidence. He's the one fighting for your son". She is floored and speechless as Court exits. She immediately calls the Chief and demands an explanation. "Why isn't the entire department all over this? Why does my husband's arch nemesis seem to be the only one interested in clearing my son?" The Chief has no answers. The Chief naturally wants and demands answers from the command staff, after all, he ordered McGuire to stay away from the case. McGuire's boss' back him 100 percent, finally. They assure the Chief that McGuire did pass the case on and that others were working it.

Court returns to McGuire and tells him what he learned or lack thereof. He explains the early morning phone call between Bucci and his son. He tells McGuire about the time of 0447. McGuire pauses and doesn't realize right away why that doesn't seem to fit. *Why does that seem like a mistake?* He grabs the folder and flips through the file and comes to a page with a still photo of the bear den just as the bears begin to exit. The time stamp is exactly 0430. Assuming that the time stamp is accurate and set correctly, what are the chances that he is still alive and has access to his phone? If he's fucked up on this poison dart voodoo drug shit, or even if he's combined it with another substance, shouldn't he already be in the pit? Even if they follow the theory that maybe he dropped his phone over the ledge and tried to re-trieve it. He'd have to at the very least be in the fight for his life right now. These times do not add up. At 0430, these animals are out of their cave and in the exhibit with him.

"So who the fuck is using his phone and do we know what was said?" asks McGuire. "We don't" replies Court. "His wife said that the Major uttered the phrase "sins of the father or sons of the father" a few times and nodded off. But he explains that apparently that was common with the Major's fucked up sleep patterns in the months before his death. "Sins of the father? Is he mad at his father?" McGuire thinks out loud. Even so, the timing is off. McGuire is convinced that this is in fact a homicide. And that the killer used Bucci Jr's phone.

27

The Connection

McGuire is now on a mission. If this is the last case he will ever work, he's gonna get it right. With still nothing to go on, he asks for consent to the phones of everyone at the Broad St firehouse as well as the zoo employees. All comply with the new understanding that this is a homicide investigation. The phones are dumped and none hit off the cell towers closest to the zoo on that morning at the correct time. He goes over case notes when he's notified that the toxicology results arrive after the Detective Commander demanded a rush be put on them. As he suspects, no other substances are found in his body.

Kenny ponders out loud "isn't it strange that the Chief and his number 2 lose both their sons in fucked up circumstances just a few months apart?" *Holy shit!!* McGuire forgot all about the Chief's boy. It was on the eve of his trial and he was still suspended, he never made it to the scene.

"Where's that case?" he asks. "What case?" Court responds, "the Chief closed it that night. It's off-limits and even I'm not gonna touch that one for you". Nonetheless, Jason calls the night detectives that responded, looking for similarities in the crime scene. Were there syringes nearby? Most city parks were littered with them, although not necessarily the elite east side. That wouldn't be common and therefore a smoking gun if one was found. No one recalled seeing any evidence of drug paraphernalia at the scene, just plenty of evidence of drinking.

He walks down to the BCI office and convinces a detective to let him see the crime scene photos. The detective is reluctant and let's McGuire know that he's on his own. He leaves him with the file and abruptly leaves him alone in the office. Jason goes through every photo. Studying each one at length. The night guys recollected correctly. No needles. He looks at photos taken of the colonel's son. One taken from a view of the inside of his mouth shows a clear entrance wound in the roof, just under the nasal cavity. Exit is through the top of the head with brain matter on the ground surrounding the deceased. All consistent with a self-inflicted gun shot through the mouth. But there is something odd about one photo. It appears to have been taken about 10 feet from the deceased, looking directly at him. Jason can sense something is missing. Brandon looks like he's sleeping, at peace. Looking straight on there are no signs of trauma whatsoever. *"Where's the blood?"* he thinks. There should be blood everywhere. His entire naval cavity was destroyed. He should have bled out of his nose and mouth for several seconds to even minutes after the shot ripped through his head. He should have bled severely until the heart finally stopped pumping. At least that is what normally happens. The heart normally wouldn't have stopped right away. He leans back in the chair and closes his eyes.

A Vision

I scout the area and learn Feldman's habits. Where he hangs. Where he scores his junk. I notice that he likes to go out late at night for a nightcap of smack in the park. I wait for him, maybe posing as another user. I tell him I got some good shit, some REAL shit. He naturally begs for a taste. I give him some. The dumb fuck injects it himself and almost instantly goes numb. He can't move. But those eyes, they show fear. He's knows something isn't right but he can't do anything. Can't run. Can't cry out. The plan is to now follow it up with a shot of legit heroin with a few doses of Narcan readily available. I'm gonna give him is magic poison and pull him out of his high over and over again. And after four of five times, hit him with a dose of pure smack, killing him instantly. Torture! An intentional overdose from an obvious junky. But something goes wrong. His eyes go blank. They're not moving anymore. His chest isn't rising. What the fuck…..he's not breathing. Shit! He's not going to feel the pain. My plan is shot. Plan B. I place the barrel of the gun in his mouth, using his own hand to cradle the handle for GSR. I let a round go and let the gun fall. I'm gone.

The Big Break

And the thoughts come all too easy, frightening himself in the process. He waits in the office until the BCI lieutenant arrives. Seeing the file spread out in front of him, she explodes.

"What the fuck are you doing in this office with that file? That case is closed and off limits on the Chief's orders".

"Lou, hear me out please" Jason says.

He knows that they don't normally see eye to eye and have had their differences. He goes over the photos with her and about the lack of blood. After several minutes, he convinces her that it appears odd. But most cases do. Every case is different. Just when you think they become routine, bam, you see something new. Forensics is an ever-changing profession. Each case has to be attacked based on the evidence provided. He begs her to allow him access to the evidence gathered. There are beer and soda cans and bottles scattered in close proximity to the body, cigarette butts everywhere.

He asks that they be processed for prints and then sent out for DNA analysis. She is reluctant, asking what would prints or DNA found on any piece of evidence prove. It would only place someone at the park at any given time and not necessarily the time of the suicide. Jason presses, and admits that it is a long shot. A one in a million chance. But what if this is a murder? What if the same person or people killed Brandon and Sergio? Feldman after all was responsible for the firing of several police officers.

She refuses. She won't get in the Chiefs crosshairs based on wild assumptions. Especially with a Captain's exam coming up, those additional "Chief's" points become extremely valuable. "This isn't Hollywood kid". "Maybe it's more Hollywood than you think, Lieutenant" he says. He explains the evidence and the what ifs. We know chrono-logically that this incident happened way before Bucci's. What if this was the suspect's first at-tempt at using the anesthetic? What if he didn't realize how fast-acting it was and before he could torture or kill Brandon, he stopped breathing. If he stopped breathing long before the shot, his heart would have stopped. This would explain the lack of blood. And the Chief fucked it all up, refusing the autopsy. The Lieutenant doesn't bring it up, but she can't stop thinking about the note that sent the Chief into a tailspin which resulted in him clos-ing the case file immediately. If McGuire knew about the note, he'd be convinced it was staged.

But if she told him about the note, he'd surely confront the Chief. No-one wanted to know what was in that note.

"Now look at Bucci. Different manner of death no doubt. But the respirator. This sick fuck wanted to torture him. And after realizing that he needed breathing apparatus after the Feldman case, he brought it with him. He left it at the scene. Feldman was his first. It was like a trial run".

The lieutenant thought he was nuts. The one thing he was lacking was motive. Either than every cop on and off the job, who the fuck would want to hurt both Feldman and Bucci? No cop would do it, not to the boss' family members. Cops have long hated their chiefs and command staff. It's part of the job. They don't fucking kill them or their kids for it.

But she is convinced, no matter how movie like it seemed, that something was there. Jason's wild fucked-up imagination was being put to good use once again. She told him that she would send the items out, even under her name. But swore to him that if she got caught, she'd kill him with her own two hands. McGuire waits patiently for weeks.

He finally gets a call from the lieutenant asking him to respond to her office. He's on a day off but rushes in anyway. She explains that prints were lifted on a few of the bottles and cans. She shows him the results and as he flips through them, he comes across a specific name, Daniel Thomas. He falls out of the chair to the floor. He's still semi-conscious as she calls for help. Before passing out, he calls out "Uncle Danny".

30

A Total Nightmare

Jason spends the next month at RI Mental Health after suffering a major nervous breakdown. How could one guy take on so much stress? One fucked up thing after another. He's ruled unfit for duty and placed out of work on injury status.

He's fucked up on all sorts of meds. Depression. Anxiety. Anti-seizure. He can only watch the news from his room. He watches in horror as Danny is perp-walked into and out of the station and into court. He watches as Chief Feldman holds his press conference. He honors the men involved in capturing the killer of his son and of Patrolman Bucci. They're lauded as heroes. He talks about their non-stop effort. How they never gave up. Frank Ventura is identified as the lead detective. Live on the evening news the colonel awards Ventura with the Chief's Award. He also awards it to Ventura's sergeant, lieutenant, and captain although neither of them had anything to do with the case.

Jason reads the papers and sees that Danny gave it up. He gave a complete statement. A search warrant conducted on his apartment found him to be hiding a bottle of d-tubocurarine extract with a bag of syringes between his mattresses. It is explained how Ventura single-handedly traced the portable respirator back to the Broad St firehouse where Danny hung out and sometimes slept. The stories would go on about Danny's troubled life and his unpredictable temper. Jason couldn't bear it. He was in a fog.

After a month he went straight home. He didn't leave his house for 60 straight days. Hardly ate. Hardly showered. He was popping pills at an alarming rate. And hitting the bottle, hard. Anything to get his mind elsewhere. If at any time Jason was hoping for another ass-kicking and concussion, now was it. This was his fault. Not Danny's. Maybe he wasn't clear enough in telling him to lay off of his thoughts of revenge. He never thought Danny was serious.

How could he return to work? Danny was family. Danny did this for Jason. It was the same as Jason doing the crime himself. Now he wish he had. He was going to feel the brunt of the blame anyway, even if it was only in his imagination. He'd wipe out the entire Feldman and Bucci bloodlines if it could save Danny. He knew he would be examining everyone's eyes as they glanced at him. If they glanced at him at all. He was in the deepest depression of his life. One he saw no way out of.

31

Closing Time

After the third month, he convinced his doctors and The Job to let him back in the squad in a light duty capacity. He caught a high from this job and just wanted to be there one last time. To see it and feel it. He wouldn't catch any new cases. It was closing time. He just wanted to close out what he already had and then retire. He was officially checked out.

The Job was unexpectedly warm to him though. Most knew him and knew he would have never taken part in this. It was a great relief to him to know that. He would want to look at Danny's file, but couldn't bring himself to. He did read the final narrative in the report though which indicated that Danny's response to every question was "I hurt them". Not quite a confession, but enough to run with when you have a feeble-minded defendant. Jason sat for hours just trying to piece together the circumstances. He knew the who and the why. But he couldn't figure out the how.

How could Danny do this? He was severely mentally handicapped. He had two brain cells that were constantly battling one another. Even if he found the anesthetic at his job in the hospital, how the fuck would he even know what it was or what it did? Did Danny have murder in him? Possibly. But not this kind it seemed. This was a thinking man's murder. Danny had the physical ability to rip these guys apart and no amount of bullets would stop him. But that's not what happened here.

Although sick to think that way, it would have been an easier pill to swallow and easier to understand if they had been fatally beaten. He wants to see Danny but can't bring himself to go. Jason has so many questions, but most of them he truly doesn't want to know the answer to. He's done investigating. He's done trying to put pieces of a puzzle together. His brain has slowed to a halt. He's numb to the world.

Feeling his son's mental torture, his father tries to get him out of the house. A game of golf here and there. A cigar or two. Dinner a couple nights a week. Finally Jason opens up to his father. Dennis knew Danny best. How did he view the case? Does he think Danny had it in him? Could Jay have done anything to prevent this? His father truly doesn't know and is at a loss for an explanation. On one hand, he saw Danny as harmless, only reacting when presented with a real threat and Danny hadn't acted out in years. Did he have the mental capability to pull something like this off?

Jason thinks that this could easily be a setup, with all the physical evidence planted. " More than likely not on his own" Dennis explained. "But you remember back to when you were a kid? Cop shows. NYPD Blue. Forensic Files. Now he's been watching CSI and all that other bullshit. Remember he could watch a show once and recite it word for word. He was like the fucking Rain Man". Could that have been it? The missing link? Could he have gotten this idea from some stupid television show and acted it out? It still was too far fetched for Jason to believe. But so was everything these days.

They take a long ride back to Jason's house to drop him off. On the ride, his father finally opens up to him after all these years about Woodhaven Boys Home. He talks about the horror inflicted on everyone there. No one left unhurt. No one left untouched. It was a pedophiles dream. No one escaped the torture, including him and his siblings. That was the type of place that could easily drive someone to kill Dennis explained. And they both know Danny was there the longest. No-one that went there could possibly be held at fault for anything they did if people knew the true stories.

The Job

He breaks out in tears, something Jason had never seen before. His invincible father. More popular than Bo Duke. Crying like a baby. Uncontrollably for about 15 minutes. It was the most surreal moment in Jason's memory which has been full of fucked up moments in recent years. He finally comes to and apologizes to Jay. Jason doesn't know what to say. But he knows what his dad loves most.

"Hey, how 'bout some golf and cigars in the morning?" Jason asks.

"Sure kid". "I'll set up a 10 o'clock tee time. Pick you up around 9:30. And don't forget to bring balls this time and mark them. You've been losing them left and right" Dennis said.

"Ok dad".

32

Finally, Peace at Last

It was a night of soul-searching for Jason. Smoking. Watching his son in the pool. He was trying to find a way to come to terms with what happened as well as his pending early retirement. Hearing the detail in which his father described the boys' home made it seem like it was more than enough to make a man kill. Some have killed for a lot less. It helped him to find a little inner peace and closure. And he needed to find a new job. But that was the least of his worries for now.

The following morning he woke earlier than normal. Like he used to before his Christmas Eve beating. Like a normal person. He grabs his clubs and leaves the house around 8:30. Jason calls his father and tells him he'll meet him at the golf course, that he has something to take care of first. He drives over to the hospital unit of the corrections' intake center and calls a friend from the prison's Special Investigative Unit. It's time to see Danny. Even if only once.

The investigator sets them up in a cozy office. They sit across from each other and gaze silently. Jason has so many questions, but won't ask. He

knows what the response will be, "I hurt them".
Danny seems happy and healthy. Happier than
Jason has ever seen him. The poor guy had been
in and out of institutions his entire life. Maybe in
some fucked-up way, this was home to him. He
clearly suffered from Institutional Syndrome. It
was certainly a paradise compared to Woodhaven.
Nothing is said for about 30 minutes.

Jason doesn't openly sob but can't stop the obvious tears from rolling down his cheeks. He
walks over to Danny and gets grabbed in a bear
hug. He tells him he loves his "Uncle". And
thanks him. Danny replies "I love you too". And
that was it. He exits the facility and explodes in a
thunderous cry in his car. Enough to get the attention of passersby. *Why would I thank Danny?* It's
clear to him now, that he is satisfied. Content with
life. And fully giving in to his feelings for once.
Their kid's are dead. So the fuck what? They
wanted him to hurt, to suffer. To do the unthink-
able to himself or maybe someone else. They
wanted his father to be without his son. And they
wanted his son to be without his father. Karma.
Sweet karma, you sick fucks. Yeah, he gave their
son's cases everything he had, but that was The
Job. That was HIS job. And he did his job.

And just like that, it's over. The pain that began
a few years earlier on that Christmas Eve is now

officially gone. His breathing is easier. His smile is wider. On his way to the country club, he pours his meds out of the window on the highway.

He and Dennis hookup and begin stretching and taking practice swings.

"Did you take care of that thing" Dennis asks.

"Yup, I went and saw Uncle Danny" Jason responds.

"Oh, what did he have to say?" Dennis says looking puzzled and nervous.

"Absolutely nothing" Jason replies with a smile.

"What's with the smile, kid? I haven't seen that in years. Don't start getting all normal on me now" Dennis jokes.

"I feel good" Jason says, "as good as I've felt in a long time".

"Did you remember to pick up some balls?" Dennis asks.

"Fuck me" Jason screams, "I totally forgot".

"Jesus" says Dennis, "don't worry, I have some extra."

He hands Jason a half dozen balls and a permanent marker.

"Put an X through my marker so we know it's yours."

Jason rolls the first ball around until he finds his

father's mark.

"I-14:21, what the heck does that mean"?
"Nothing. Just something I figured would be unique. Had to change it up a little" his father responds.

Jason seems to not remotely know of or understand its meaning. He crosses out the mark and it's time to play through.

Jason tees up his first shot. A few practice swings and WACK!! The ball naturally travels two fairways to the right.

Dennis says "oh, you're definitely back to normal now".
"Thanks Dad, for everything, I mean that"

And as if on cue, they simultaneously wink.

A Personal Plea

This message is for all my brothers and sisters in LE. But not simply for them. It's for anyone who has suffered from PTSD or Post-Concussion Syndrome or any type of brain related injury. The message is:

DON'T DO IT!!!

There. That's it. Thanks for spending your hard-earned cash on my book.

But seriously....Don't do it. Life is precious. Every life has meaning, even if you can't see or feel that meaning in your very own life. I'm obviously not a doctor, but I can speak from experience and what helped for me.

Listening to all the experts and reading all the literature on the matter, I kind of took a little info from each in my approach. Most believe PTSD applies simply to military action. Far from it. It often occurs in law enforcement and yes, even those nitwit firefighters (BOOM!!!). It also can happen to any person in any profession or walk of life. A woman being sexually assaulted will often get PTSD based on a location and be fearful of parking lots or stairwells. It happens to anyone in a serious situation in which death for that person is a great possibility.

Now, some would say that they've been in that situation numerous times and have never felt the after effects. Fine. You're a tough guy. A major badass. Go fuck yourself. What is that A-type personality going to do for you in the afterlife? I myself have been involved in several life threatening situations. As a Major Crimes detective, I have seen the most awful part of what the human soul is capable of. Never was I affected to the point where I couldn't leave my home simply to go food shopping. I was never mentally tortured to the point that I stayed in bed for days at a time.

That all changed after I had my son. I still did my job. I was still brave as hell. But I decided to use my brain just a little bit more. I made it a point to look for escape routes as I approached danger. Gone were the rookie days of being gung-ho. But as we all know in law enforcement, trouble will eventually find you. Somehow, someway.

My issues occurred after my son was born. After I truly gave a fuck about living. Immediately following a brutal beating that left me a total mess, consciously I felt fine. There were several aggressors and I still made it out alive with what I thought was a minor bang to the head. That had to count for something. I truly believed in the fact that getting back up after being knocked down was the true meaning of toughness. Not how hard you can hit. In that moment, I wasn't aware of what this beat-down was actually doing to me internally. This concussion shit which is now the hottest topic in all contact sports is real. What I didn't fully realize because it was deep in my subconscious, was that I knew that I almost died. And leaving my son truly terrified me. Not that he couldn't make it without me. But because I couldn't make it without him. Yes, even in heaven. I am a God fearing man. I do believe in the afterlife and the beauty that awaits. But I don't think I could last a day in heaven, with all of its glory, without my son. I truly feel that way. I would go through hell with him for an eternity rather than spend one day in heaven without him.

That fear of leaving my son caused my PTSD and took my brain on a rollercoaster ride that I may never fully recover from. So what did I do? What should you do? Again, I'm not a doctor. No formal education after high school in fact. I'm just a guy and can only speak to you from my experiences. And my message again is: don't do it. First and foremost, find medical help. It's out there now. Years ago it was seen as a sign of weakness for LEO's to seek severe psychiatric help. It's not like that anymore. It's common knowledge that more LEO's die from suicide each year than are murdered by a felon in the line of duty. And don't do it for the sake of the job. Don't do it to avoid being a liability. Fuck the job. Especially in this day and age. Your brass would sell you out in a minute. This is not about saving your thankless job. Do it for you. For your family. For your friends. For the people you serve. And when you're in that situation, you truly feel that you have no friends and no support.

So pick something. Anything. There are a million reasons to live and get better. Whether it's seeing Tom Brady win another Super Bowl. Or staying alive long enough to see the next Star Wars release. Pick some inspiration. There has to be something you love. You might think I'm making an attempt at humor, I'm not. When I was in my deepest depression, the context of my life was all fucked up. I couldn't see my support system. I was homeless for a time and living in a friend's borrowed van. Not down by the river like Matt Foley either. And not because my family didn't want to help, I didn't want their help.

But there were other things, maybe not attached to me deeply, that always brought me pleasure even in my darkest moments. So yes, football, movies, great cigars, motorcycles etc... All things that made me smile, I focused on. Waiting for the next great cigar release two months from now. BOOM...two more months alive. Star Wars next Christmas. Gotta live long enough to see it right? As stupid as this sounds, this is what I did. I searched and searched for what may seem to you the reader as the stupidest things to hold on to. But what you and I draw as inspiration and reasons for living are totally different things.

It's hard to search for truly deep reasons to believe in so choose the little ones. The ones that aren't so obvious. It could be anything to anyone. Why not choose my son? Because that was too simple a choice, I think. When you feel as fucked up and as worthless as I did, I truly felt at times that my son was better off with me gone. It was too close to my heart. I found myself thinking about his needs and what's best for him and I couldn't put it all into context. Naturally he's the reason I did it. But if I needed an outside push, what's better than Brady and Belichik?

Song too. This is the corniest of reasons but you've always heard about the power of music. Like poetry, songs can take you to a different place. Millions of songs are packed with great meaning. Like every fucking country song ever! Pick one or two or several. My personal favorite was 'Original of the Species' by U2. I once heard that the song was written by the band for their children. Whether it was or wasn't didn't matter. I was convinced it was made for my son. I'd listen to that song on a loop nonstop when I was in my car with pictures of my son all over the dash. If that's what is needed, how stupid can that be?

But besides your reasons for inspiration, seek medical help. And keep seeking it until you find help that you can realize immediately. And don't turn to booze. Whatever you do, don't self-medicate with alcohol. You don't feel it while in the middle of a drunken stupor, but it's making matters worse. We've all heard that a million times and for some stupid reason we still do it. So I can't waste much time on the booze subject. I can only be one more of the gazillion voices that says don't drink.

I saw several doctors that were hacks. They went through their motions and gave me the same protocol procedures as everyone that visited their practice. They were like robots. Pump you with meds and "I'll see you in two months". TWO FUCKING MONTHS!!! I just told you that I was done with life so you simply increase my meds and send me on my own for two months? Then I found the right doctor. He set me straight with one visit. What did he do? He took out a model of the human brain. He showed me the hippocampus, the prefrontal cortex, and the amygdala. No,

I didn't make those names up. He explained how
they work and how they were being affected due
to my issues. He explained how one messed with
my fight or flight response. How one made me re-
act when in large crowds. How after going to just
about every New England Patriots game for 17
years, I could no longer go. Something about being in large crowds with people that had been
drinking heavily caused me to panic
uncontrollably. Why? Because I was attacked by
a large drunken group.

What was most important, was that he explained to me that I was absolutely NORMAL.
Completely normal. Somehow knowing that this is
exactly the way I was supposed to feel under the
circumstances made me realize that I was not a
goner. The endless nasty thoughts that entered
my mind as I lay in bed at night were not a sign
that I was going fucking batshit nuts, it was simply
how I was supposed to think. He explained that
as the weeks and months went on, my thoughts
would change to this or that. And they did, exactly
as he said they would. I was normal. For me, the
hardest part of my ordeal psychologically was truly
believing that I was crazy and a danger to others.
Sitting there thinking nonstop that you are crazy
will have you convinced that you are. Once convinced that I was thinking normally, everything
changed. I could anticipate my thoughts and my

mood. I knew when I would make awful company and turned down invitations to events. I knew when it was time to take in a good comedy.

The hardest part was convincing myself not to drink. No foreign substance except for prescribed medication can help. And even when that doesn't work, reach back on your inspirations. Those things that bring you good thoughts. Get out of the house. Take up golf. Treat yourself to an expensive cigar. Did I mention Tom Brady? If you have children, spend every free minute you have with them. But spend that time with them out of the house. I felt the strongest demons were at home. While there, I had nothing to do but think. And believe me, while suffering PTSD or concussion issues, you cannot control your thoughts. They will automatically go to shit. So take day trips with them. The beach maybe. Fenway Paahhhhk!! Movies or picnics. Watch them run and play. Try to get into their minds and live there for a while. Try to see what they see and think the way they do.

I am not an expert in this. But my brothers and sisters in blue know the one major rule to the job: everyone goes home. That is what we were told day one. But that is not enough for me. What happens when our brothers and sisters are at home? We need to make sure they also make it back to that next shift. And to make sure that they eventually retire after a long and fulfilling career. It is true that this is the worst and best profession that ever existed. Safety, both physical and mental for our members is the key. We owe it to each other. We owe to our families. We owe it to the people we serve. To be of sound mind at all times. Even though we are human, we can't afford to be. Always remember, you will fall. Get your ass back up and continue, both on and off The Job. That is the true meaning of toughness, not a meaningless bench press.

Be safe out there.

Made in the USA
Middletown, DE
31 May 2016